'A long overdue and highly accessible contribution to the field of family violence that addresses the previously neglected needs of its youngest victims. Dr Wendy Bunston places at centre stage the experience of infants and children, offering both a theoretical underpinning of her approach and a hands-on repertoire of therapeutic interventions that will prove invaluable to both early career and seasoned clinicians alike.'

– Fiona True LCSW, Co-Director, Center for Children and Relational Trauma, Ackerman Institute for the Family, New York, USA

'Dr Bunston's infant-led approach is an exceptional resource for practitioners working at the front line of family violence services. It provides a coherent, strategic set of principles with sufficient detailed case study material to make sense of the complex and multi-layered experience of interpersonal violence. The theoretical material is written in a particularly accessible style but the real punch comes in taking apart the examples of "adult-centric" thinking. I repeatedly found myself reacting in surprise at how I too could easily overlook the experience of the infant in trying to understand the actions of fathers in troubled families. The book also reflects Wendy's generous caring approach in that she offers ways for the practitioner to be "looked after" while engaging the family through infant-led work.'

– Dr Richard Fletcher, Associate Professor, Family Action Centre, University of Newcastle, Australia

'Providing extensive offerings of real-life clinical examples, this book not only changes the way we think about infants, but actively promotes a new way of practising. It's not a manual, it's a philosophy of practice that has been long awaited in this field.'

– Angelique Jenny PhD, Wood's Homes Research Chair in Children's Mental Health, Faculty of Social Work, University of Calgary, Canada

D1548329

of related interest

Making an Impact – Children and Domestic Violence
A Reader
Marianne Hester, Chris Pearson and Nicola Harwin with Hilary Abrahams
ISBN 978 1 84310 157 4
eISBN 978 1 84642 584 4

Talking to My Mum
A Picture Workbook for Workers, Mothers and Children Affected by Domestic Abuse
Cathy Humphreys, Ravi K. Thiara, Agnes Skamballis and Audrey Mullender
ISBN 978 1 84310 422 3
eISBN 978 1 84642 526 4

Helping Children to Tell about Sexual Abuse
Guidance for Helpers
Rosaleen McElvaney
ISBN 978 1 84905 712 7
eISBN 978 1 78450 235 5

Healing Child Trauma through Restorative Parenting
A Model for Supporting Children and Young People
Dr Chris Robinson and Terry Philpot
Forewords by Andrew Constable and Karen Mitchell-Mellor
ISBN 978 1 84905 699 1
eISBN 978 1 78450 215 7

Learning through Child Observation, Third Edition
Mary Fawcett and Debbie Watson
ISBN 978 1 84905 647 2
eISBN 978 1 78450 141 9

Direct Work with Family Groups
Simple, Fun Ideas to Aid Engagement and Assessment and Enable Positive Change
Audrey Tait and Helen Wosu
ISBN 978 1 84905 554 3
eISBN 978 0 85700 986 9

How Are You Feeling Today Baby Bear?
Exploring Big Feelings After Living in a Stormy Home
Jane Evans
Illustrated by Laurence Jackson
ISBN 978 1 84905 424 9
eISBN 978 0 85700 793 3

An Integrative Approach to Treating Babies and Children
A Multidisciplinary Guide
Edited by John Wilks
ISBN 978 1 84819 282 9
eISBN 978 0 85701 229 6

Helping Babies and Children Aged 0–6
to Heal After Family Violence

A Practical Guide to Infant- and Child-Led Work

Dr Wendy Bunston

FOREWORD BY DR JULIE STONE

Jessica Kingsley *Publishers*
London and Philadelphia

First published in 2017
by Jessica Kingsley Publishers
73 Collier Street
London N1 9BE, UK
and
400 Market Street, Suite 400
Philadelphia, PA 19106, USA

www.jkp.com

Library of Congress Cataloging in Publication Data
Names: Bunston, Wendy, author.
Title: Helping babies and children aged 0-6 to heal after family violence : a
    practical guide to infant- and child-led work / Dr. Wendy Bunston.
Description: London ; Philadelphia : Jessica Kingsley Publishers, [2017] |
    Includes bibliographical references.
Identifiers: LCCN 2016056016 | ISBN 9781849056441 (alk. paper)
Subjects: LCSH: Victims of family violence--Services for. | Child welfare. |
    Child psychotherapy. | Social work with children.
Classification: LCC HV6626 .B86 2017 | DDC 362.82/923--dc23 LC record available at
https://lccn.loc.gov/2016056016

British Library Cataloguing in Publication Data
A CIP catalogue record for this book is available from the British Library

ISBN 978 1 84905 644 1
eISBN 978 1 78450 138 9

Printed and bound in the United States

This book is dedicated to my greatest teachers: the infants, children and young people who have taught me how to follow their lead. And to my first teachers, my parents Sally and Ocky, my aunties Gwinny and Judy, and my constant companion in life, Ruth.

Contents

Foreword

For those of us who work with infants, young children and their families, Dr Wendy Bunston's book is a gift. In it Wendy offers an overview of the current knowledge of neurodevelopment and the indelible impact of early trauma. She also distils the essence of her learning and her experience. Her experience comes from decades of tireless and courageous work to bring greater understanding and compassion to the reality of family violence and its effect on each and every one of us.

Wendy's clinical practice and her research have focused on broadening the limits of traditional ways of thinking about young children. She inspires us to find new ways to address and redress the potentially devastating consequences that family violence has on the lives of children aged 0–6.

Wendy speaks and writes with a clear voice as a champion for our youngest and most vulnerable. It has been my privilege to work alongside Wendy, to learn from her, to marvel at her keen intelligence, to be inspired by her capacity to see beyond the status quo that seeks to limit, tidy-up or dismiss the messy, distressing and frightening. Wendy does not shy away from the difficult; she faces it head-on.

In this book, she offers her own thinking to embolden other practitioners' thinking and clinical practice. Wendy brings energy, playfulness and humour to her work and to her writing. Her wisdom brings leaven to the tough minute-to-minute experience of children and families who have lived with family violence, and to those of us who strive to engage with and make a difference to children whose lives have been scarred by the experience of family violence.

This book is one to read and to share with colleagues who work with families, regardless of their discipline or their role. In finding creative ways to confront the issue of family violence, there is much to learn from this book and there is something here for us all.

Julie Stone, BA, BM, FRAZCP
Infant, Child and Family Psychiatrist,
Fellow of Zero to Three, Washington,
Founding Director of the Uthando Project, working for
the children of Kwa-Zulu Natal, South Africa
November 2016

Acknowledgments

I cannot thank Dr Julie Stone enough for all her wisdom, insight, support and feedback throughout the writing of this book. I also thank Shannon Sproule for his wonderful artwork in creating the umbrella cartoons in Chapter Six and Susannah Duncan for her kind assistance with the diagram used in Chapter Three. I am grateful to the many passionate and compassionate colleagues over the past three decades who have worked with me in creating some important therapeutic interventions and opportunities to truly advocate for the voice of infants and children. Lastly, I am very grateful and pleased to have been given permission to make use of the wonderful picture used for the front cover of this book. Its meaning is both very personal and poignant, and I am thankful for being allowed the opportunity to celebrate a magical childhood moment, and memory.

Introduction

Infants and young children are at the centre of, and are the reason for, having written this book. Relational violence in the homes of infants and children is all too common. How we best, and safely, attend to the emotional, psychological and relational world of the infant and child growing up in such contexts, is often neither well considered nor well serviced. This is even though infants and young children are more likely to be present during family violence incidents and are more vulnerable to harm than any other age group. Yet infants and small children are the least likely to be directly responded to, provided with specialist support and services, or recognised as the most receptive to positive change. This book hopes to change that reality. This is not necessarily through an increased demand for funding, although that would be both appropriate and advantageous. If serviced differently, however, I believe the outcomes of infant- and child-led practice would result in dramatic changes and benefits to how the family violence sector, and society generally, responds to and heals from family violence.

This book is aimed at changing that part of the system which responds at the front line: ourselves. This is workers, foster carers, nurses, counsellors, teachers and all other professionals who do the 'hands-on' work with infants, children and families. We can encourage change from the ground up. This is through taking our lead from, and advocating for, the youngest members of the families impacted by family violence. This does not necessarily require additional money. This takes additional time, and a change in how we think about, reflect on and undertake our practice. This book will offer a guide to how infant- and child-led practice is undertaken within the context of family violence. Case examples are provided throughout to illustrate how this approach has been used in practice. Infant- and child-led approaches are organic. They are also committed to keeping infants and young children protected and valued within all aspects of their rapidly developing emotional and bio-neurological self, and caregiving world. The baby in utero, through to the young child, is considered. How to bring the subjectivity of infant and child alive, and the need to recognise and employ the potential, hope and healing the newborn brings, even within the context of violence, is thoroughly canvassed.

This book brings together the theory and research which informs an infant- and child-led approach, what fundamental practice principles are important, and how we expand the way we think about what leads to growth and healing. Group work, family work, working with adults and various other interventions are discussed. The importance of other caregiving systems such as foster care and women's refuges are also highlighted. Crucial to this approach is enhancing our ability to use our reflective selves, and recognising the importance of accessing reflective supervision to support and enhance our work within such a complex and challenging arena of practice. This is a book about healing, and about hope, and honouring the world of the infant and young child, and the families with whom they are so profoundly connected.

Chapter One

It is emotionally confronting to fully engage with the anxious and vulnerable infant, particularly when we know that they live in an environment where they may be in harm's way. So, we often don't. We hope that by intervening with the parent we can tend to the child. This may take a considerable amount of time, and even resistance, where a parent has experienced substantial trauma, and over many years. It seldom occurs to us that by attending to the child we may be throwing the parent a lifeline they would not otherwise have considered accepting.

Not 'Throwing the Baby Out with the Bathwater'

'How did a loving mother come to kill her own child?' This headline caught my attention in an Australian newspaper (Stafford 2016). The article described how two-year-old Amy was drowned by her mother, and the details of this story have haunted me ever since. Family violence was evidently not involved, but Amy's life ended in violence. It was a story about how a small girl appeared to be left to emotionally manage on her own while her mother became increasingly unwell, and how her mother killed her. I want to use this story at the outset of this book to illustrate one of the core tenets which underpin it; that we, the adults, are not often compelled to think, express or talk about how an infant or small child might experience living with any form of relational violence. We tend to be 'adult centric', not seeing the world through the child's eyes, but through the eyes of their parents, or ourselves.

Fully engaging with an infant or young child's psychological distress is often too confronting and too painful. Yet, if we are not prepared to go there, we leave the very small child alone to manage this by themselves, something they are neurologically, emotionally and physiologically ill-equipped to do. Leaving infants and children alone to manage their experience of living with family violence, leaves them, metaphorically speaking, at risk of drowning.

AMY

Amy was two years old when she died. Her mother, Sarah, as reported in the newspaper article, was a devoted and adoring caregiver. They appeared to enjoy a very close and loving relationship for the first 18 months of Amy's life. Amy's father Arlo stated that Sarah 'absolutely adored' Amy, and she 'was a very very good mother' (Stafford 2016, p.30). Further, he is quoted as saying that 'Amy had an awesome life. She had a golden life. Every moment of her life was good' (p.31). However, in the six months before Amy was drowned in a dam, her mother had become increasingly paranoid and was sliding into psychosis. Multiple times Sarah fled the family home with Amy, going to her parents, friends or neighbours. Sarah believed that she and Amy were being pursued, and that people were conspiring to harm them. Sarah's behaviour had become increasingly erratic. On one occasion, following an outburst in a public place, the police were called and Sarah was admitted to a mental health unit for a week. Presumably, this was without her daughter. Following Sarah's discharge from hospital she resisted taking her medication and hid her psychological decline from her family and friends.

Featured alongside the article were pictures of Amy, smiling and sitting on top of a slide, playing an electric organ, and a picture of the field where she had been drowned. As quoted in the article, Sarah recalled her daughter smiling up at her as she held her head under the water, then Amy's little face turning to panic. Even more gut wrenching than this was the article's concluding sentence, containing the only words attributed to Amy. Sarah states that, 'I remember getting out of the car that awful night and (how) Amy said to me, "Home mumma, home", and I wish I had listened' (Stafford 2016). The article was written to promote the completion of the first Australian Study into Filicide (when a parent kills their own child).

Not truly seeing

So, what has Amy's death got to do with infants, young children and family violence? I believe this story powerfully exemplifies how our adult-orientated society thinks of children as an appendage to their parent. Notwithstanding the enormity of the grief, guilt and condemnation Amy's mother, father and their entire family may now be feeling, this heart-breaking situation speaks to so much more. Tragically, such stories are common. During the writing of this chapter, the news-cycle in Melbourne, Australia was saturated with the story of an 18-month-old girl who was found dead in a local creek. Her mother initially reported to police that an unknown assailant had abducted the toddler when they were out walking. Three days later it was reported that the 22-year-old mother had killed her daughter. Empathy was expressed for the mother and much speculation offered by commentators as to what could have led to such a tragedy.

Again, in the very final stages of my finishing this book, the media reported on the story of a father who held a shotgun to his three-year-old daughter's head, threatening to shoot her in front of her mother. Police shot the father. There was an outpouring of support for the mother as people expressed their sympathy for her having to witness her daughter's ordeal. Fewer comments were made about what the little girl herself experienced. How many times do we read or see in the media reports of infants or toddlers harmed or killed at the hands of their parent/s, caregiver/s or a parent's new partner? This might be attributed to mental illness or some tragic accident. It may be through neglect, child abuse or family violence.

Infants and children are harmed and killed by both men and women (Bailey & Eisikovits 2014; Friedman *et al.* 2005; Osofsky 2003). It has been reliably reported across the world that infants and toddlers are the highest group of children under 15 years of age to die from abuse and neglect (AIFS 2014). While Amy's story raised very important concerns about parents struggling with serious mental health issues, the reporting of the story itself, as with so many others, appears to have viewed not just the life but the death of this toddler through the eyes of her primary caregiving adults. This speaks to an 'adult centric' approach which precludes seeing the infant, toddler or young child as a separate person, with their own feeling states, experiences and ability to communicate. Amy was the central person around which this entire story revolved. She also appeared to be, at some level, the least thought about, advocated for and heard. Understanding filicide, and in Sarah's case what led to her daughter's death, is very important. However, so too is an early recognition of what experiences children go through, as this might just prevent such devastating outcomes.

Not truly hearing

The article written about Amy supplies a considerable amount of information illustrative of many of the complexities involved in 'adult centric' thinking. This story is on the public record. The information divulged was done so with the family's consent and their names changed. No family violence was reported, however, there is little doubt that Amy experienced extremely frightening behaviours at the hands of her mother, not least during her final moments of life.

Place yourself in Amy's position. Amy was taken away from her home and her father on multiple occasions. Amy would have struggled to make sense of what her mother was saying to her and doing with her and, realistically, she would have felt her mother's anxiety and fear. How does a small child weigh up the behaviours of an increasingly unwell mother in comparison to a previously 'well' mother? The adults in this story acknowledged not grasping the full extent of Sarah's ill health, nor even entertaining the possibility of her harming Amy. Perhaps Amy, the one person who Sarah appears to have clung to and spent the most time with in those last months, knew best what anguish her mother was going through. No one appeared to ask her, nor consider what this infant was going through as she was suddenly whisked off to different locations. Did the mental health unit staff meet Amy during the week her mother was hospitalised? Did anyone think to ask the family what impact Sarah's behaviour was having on Amy? Did anyone truly see Amy, think to ask Amy, or ensure she was not left alone to cope with her mother's ill health?

The article was about mothers who kill their infants, not infants who are killed by their mothers. The adults took the lead in this story and Amy was lost. Had the mental health professionals who dealt with Sarah, the police officers who escorted her to the unit, the other adults (family, friends and neighbours) seen Amy as not the dearly loved child of Sarah, but a person in her own right, the outcome may have been different. I have purposefully presented this story about a mother, and not a father who harms their child. Just as we tend to assume it is men who usually harm, rather than women (regardless of the circumstances), we need to take nothing for granted when operating from a perspective which, as will be detailed later, is intentionally 'infant-led', to overt that infants and children do indeed have a perspective.

THE BABY AND THE BATHWATER

The title of 'Not "Throwing the Baby Out with the Bathwater"' emphasises the objective of this first chapter and the book overall. This book is not about what we throw out but what we keep. The title refers to an old and popular saying, 'don't throw the baby out with the bathwater'. This old saying was about unwittingly throwing out something good (the baby) with something bad (the dirty water). This book is about throwing neither the baby nor the bathwater out. This book is about finding what is good in the baby and what is good in the waters (the caregiving environment) surrounding the baby, as both are important. It is also about recognising the very real risks the baby or child is exposed to in their caregiving environments when violence is present. Small babies and small children are highly vulnerable to unfavourable conditions in their environment. The infant is dependent on their caregiving system. To continue the analogy with the caregiving environment, the baby exposed to bathwater which is too hot will burn, too cold will chill, and left alone, could and on occasion will drown.

This work is not hazard free. It is fraught, and our job as adults and as workers is to ensure that the safety of the infant and very young children remains paramount (see Chapter Three). What this work offers, however, is the possibility of capitalising on hope, and seeing the infant or small child as a potential entry point for change in working to address family violence.

THREE CENTRAL THEMES

There are three central themes which lay the foundation for this book, and which underpin everything that is discussed throughout. These are:

- the impact of 'adult centric' thinking and practices

- infant-led approaches (in utero through to approximately two-year-olds)

- child-led approaches (approximately two- to six-year-olds).

The first of these themes involves 'adult centric' thinking and practices (as already referred to) which privilege the perspective of the adult at the expense of the child. The two subsequent themes are 'infant-led' and 'child-led' approaches in intervening where there is or has been family violence. These infant- and child-led approaches operate from the same premise but diverge developmentally in some important ways. Neither approach advocates precluding the perspective of significant others (parents, older siblings, alternative caregivers), as will be fully explained. Later in this chapter I will explain my preference for the use of the term 'family violence' over other descriptors, and what this term encompasses within the context of this book. Finally, significant to any discussion about family violence is the recognition of the gendered nature of violence. This chapter will conclude with some reflections about how the focus on gendered explanations for violence within relationships both enhances as well as clouds the level of complexity and accountability inherent in addressing the impact of violence on infants and young children.

What is 'adult centric' thinking?

We know that not all adults feel, nor are given rights which make them feel, equal. However, most adults have unequal power over children most of the time. There are often sound reasons for this, yet when this power is wielded in an unthinking, disrespectful or rigid manner, the consequences can be dire. The difference between adults making and exercising considered judgements in relation to, as well as with, children and adult centric thinking is that the latter occurs through excluding the voice of children altogether. That is, the perspective of the child is ignored, or worse still, rendered irrelevant. The presumptions operating within 'adult centric' thinking are diverse. These may include a belief that the parent or significant caregiving adult/s in the infant/child's life know, or should know, what is best. Parents in particular may consider their infant as solely their responsibility, or for some, even their property (Goodmark 1999; Maillard 2010, 2012).

There exists the belief that infants and toddlers have little to no capacity to remember, or to be adversely affected in the long term, by early traumatic events. It may be that some adults think that young children and infants cannot and do not communicate their feeling states. Often this thinking is connected to the notion that, as infants have not yet acquired language skills, they cannot express or even really know what they are feeling. Over the decades I have been working with parents, I have consistently heard them stating that their infant or child was asleep, in a different room and did not hear, or was too small to remember the violence that occurred. We know now that this is not the case. Infants are highly attuned to their environment, and they are very sensitive to and carry powerful physiological memories of trauma (Schechter & Willheim 2009; Van der Kolk 2014). This will be discussed more fully in Chapter Two. For many years, it was assumed that infants and children were either not affected by trauma or could quickly bounce back. It is true that the meanings infants attribute to frightening events are different to the meanings older children and adults give certain events. According to Rifkin-Graboi, Borelli & Enlow (2009), this is because 'infants have relatively short histories of stressful experiences' and it is more likely that their responses are driven by 'evolutionarily based pre-dispositions and other individual characteristics of the infant' (p.60). Nevertheless, infants are easily overwhelmed by frightening events and are totally dependent on their caregivers to both protect and comfort them should such events occur.

For some adults, dismissing the notion that infants feel, see, hear, taste and even associate certain smells with traumatic events can act as a defence against having to act or make changes to their lives in order to ensure the safety of their children. It is certainly less emotionally confronting to consider their infant as unaffected. Perhaps for some parents, who themselves experienced violence and trauma as children, it is easier for them to think that living with violence didn't hurt them, so neither will it hurt their children. Alternatively, their own early trauma is so deeply buried they cannot and do not want to access this. However, to believe that being adult centric in one's thinking is just something that afflicts parents, or adults who experienced early traumas themselves, is to be sorely mistaken.

Two decades ago as a newly qualified family therapist I would dread families bringing babies into a session. I feared the infant would start crying and this would distract the real work to be undertaken. I, like many workers, felt inept and anxious about including infants in my work. More than this, society in general, errs in favour of the adult over the child. Adults possess more power, status, money, resources, rights, capacities and freedoms of expression than infants and young children, even though some adults may not necessarily feel this. As has been seen repeatedly, small children are the least consulted over decisions and actions which most affect them and/or in research that concerns them (Baker 2005; Harcourt & Einarsdottir 2011; Moore *et al.* 2015; Pinheiro 2006; Waller & Bitou 2011). Effectively, they are not asked, nor listened to when they do communicate what they are feeling. The idea that infants and children can express what they want and what they need is revolutionary for some.

Challenging the idea of the child as 'entitled' or 'spoilt'

The idea of the 'spoilt' child is a phenomenon particular to Western cultures, where some children are seen to have too many rights and too few responsibilities. Giving children too much is as damaging as giving them too little. Both giving 'too little' and 'too much' suggests a parent feels that they need to keep their child at a distance. This may be because they cannot, or do not want, or do not feel they know how to adequately to give of themselves in that relationship. There are numerous possible explanations for this. The parent themselves may have experienced little intimacy as a child and now as a parent, lacks the skills, insight or confidence to offer intimacy to their child. They may feel 'over giving' is the only way to secure the love of their child. They may not have wanted their child, felt coerced or were coerced (including forced or raped) to have this child. Within the family violence literature high numbers of women report being sexually assaulted and/or being forced into pregnancy (Garcia-Moreno *et al.* 2006; McFarlane *et al.* 2005; Thiel de Bocanegra *et al.* 2010). Infant-led work in the context of rape is particularly sensitive, and needs to recognise the impact such a terrifying start to life has on the mother's perception of the child and the child's relationship experience with their mother, and their father (Thomson-Salo 2010).

There are multiple reasons for keeping children at a distance and seldom are they truly to do with wanting to spoil or punish their child. As this book will explore further, it is most often about what the parent feels they lack within themselves. It is easier to deal with such self-dislike or uncertainty by, unfortunately and unfairly, placing that hurt, betrayal or neglect on to their child rather than feeling able to deal with this within themselves. This represents adult centric thinking at its extreme. Think Miss Havisham (in Charles Dickens' *Great Expectations*), Agatha Hannigan (the orphanage supervisor in the musical *Annie* who took everything, and even Daddy Warbucks who initially gave too much) or the wicked step-mother in *Snow White* (the Grimm Brothers). Interestingly these famous depictions of adult caregivers are not biologically related to the children in their care. Might it be too hard to think that birth parent/s could or would do such things? Roald Dahl's *Matilda* does take aim at the neglectful biological parents of Matilda, but reserves the cruel and bullying headmistress Miss Trunchbull as his main target. To hold on to some fragile sense of power, the parent or caregiving adult cannot afford to see the child as needing, wanting and hungry for a relationship to which they are equally worthy of receiving and contributing.

Infant-led practice

What does an infant-led approach to working within a family violence context look like? The following chapters in this book will illustrate what this approach involves and is taken from work undertaken at the more extreme end of the spectrum. Those new to working with infants are given additional tips in Appendix One. Generally, though not always, the parents of these infants have themselves suffered enormous trauma throughout their childhood (as perhaps did their parents). In this context, being infant-led is about opening a rich but precarious channel for navigation. In my experience as a practitioner, this channel represents dangerous waters for many parents. They may have felt that they were the baby who was thrown out with the bathwater. Revisiting early memories, or imagining what it might be like to be an infant or young child, calls up deeply buried and powerfully painful emotional reminders of being at their most vulnerable. Emotional disconnection from their own past histories makes it difficult to know how to find a different way forward. Having an infant may trigger a crisis of sorts. They may imagine giving and getting the love and life they did not have. This might be their fresh start, or as one mother told me, 'having a baby might make him [i.e., her husband] change!' This sentiment is not uncommon, and can sometimes be a catalyst for change, although as workers we need to help temper placing such big expectations on such small shoulders.

Alternatively, there can be a fear of not knowing how to make things different and/or resenting their infant for demanding so much of them. Some parents may be jealous of the attention the infant takes away from them and their relationship with their partner and may see the infant as their rival, rather than as a person they can come to know, love and want to take responsibility for. Visiting some of these complex places with caregivers can be tricky, but possible and worthwhile.

The notion of being led by the infant seems a simple enough idea. It is, however, considerably harder in practice. When you work with adults who have had little attention from their caregivers, they can demand much from the working relationship. This may point to them feeling 'not heard' when young. It is important to strive for a balance. This requires holding both the caregiver/s and the infant equally in your working relationship. The idea is not to simply replace 'adult centric' thinking with 'infant centric' thinking, but inviting the infant's participation, so they can be seen, heard, and thought about. The infant or child needs and nearly always wants their caregiver. If the adult feels safely held by the working relationship, they may feel safe enough to not only tolerate but to enjoy needing their child. Working with infants requires inviting their active involvement, talking to them as you would their parent and creating pauses for discovery (read more about listening to and talking with infants in Chapter Four). It is about building a new, solid and safe relationship between both. This is done without denying that this may feel frightening, for the adult at least, as hidden feelings and thoughts are brought into awareness.

The most frail, vulnerable but newest member of their family comes ready, willing and neurologically able to reach out to build relationships (Cozolino 2008). The infant is far better at both offering and responding to invitations to relate than others. They are quicker to play, smile and move forward than adults and even older children. They can also heal more quickly, if their distress is attended to (Shatz 1992) and they are incredibly forgiving. Ultimately, they want proximity with their caregiver, even sometimes when the caregiver has been the cause of them being frightened (Main 1999). This is not to under-estimate, nor minimise, just how vulnerable infants are to their caregiving world. As will be discussed at length in Chapters Five, Six and Seven, we as workers can offer our skills to assist adults and infants impacted by family violence to experience each other and themselves in new and affirming ways.

The infant as the entry point for change

The infant as the entry point for change challenges the passivity with which many view the infant. Additionally, it calls for adults to recognise the infant's ability and right to participate in the change process. This applies as much to the infant in utero (as will be discussed in Chapter Five) as to the newborn and the toddler. Infancy can be a time when parents are prepared to seek outside assistance. Including families where there is violence, the birth of a baby very often involves contact with health professionals. Post-birth follow-up visits are expected. Where mothers are the victim of the violence, partners generally expect that their infant may need to attend a clinic regularly or perhaps even attend 'mother groups'. Professionals such as midwives, home visiting nurses or maternal child health workers are ideally placed and can have a critical impact on enabling new parents to understand how their infant is born already capable of experiencing, feeling, holding memories and communicating (Stern 2003; Van der Kolk 2014). The impact that these front-line workers have should not be under-estimated. They offer new parents a lifeline of affirmation and may be the first to help them truly see their infant. They may also be one of the few professionals allowed in by families who are suspicious of outsiders, creating the difference for vulnerable new parents being prepared to accept outside help.

In my work with running infant/mother groups to address family violence (Bunston 2006, 2008b; Bunston et al. 2016), many mothers who were still with or involved with violent partners, were free to attend our groups as their usually controlling partners believed they were meant to attend mothers' groups when the baby was so young. Many of these women informed us they would not have accessed help for themselves, but felt compelled to seek some reassurance that their infant had not been damaged by living with violence. For many, the birth of their baby had triggered their decision to leave the violent relationship. The mothers attending these groups were particularly open to using the group space to honour the experience of their infant and to learn about their child in a new and much more intimate way (Bunston *et al.* 2016). This motivation applies equally to mothers who have left violent partners and sought support from crisis accommodation services, as I will discuss further in Chapter Seven (Bunston 2016; Bunston & Glennen 2015; Bunston & Sketchley 2012).

Men who have used violence (and attended men's behaviour change programs) have also shown a commitment to attending group work (Bunston 2001, 2013b, 2015). In part, these fathers were motivated to form relationships with their children that were significantly better than the ones they experienced with their own parents. Men attending our groups described having little or no satisfaction in their relationships with their parent/s and experienced violence as they were growing up. An incentive for some fathers and mothers to address their own violence is a fear of being abandoned by their child/ren once they grow up. They may be estranged from, or do not respect or feel love towards, their own parents. This is a powerful motivator for change in their relationship with their own children, and for accepting help in how to prevent this repetition. Some parents are more afraid of not being wanted by their children once they grow up than of not being wanted by their partners. In over twenty years of working specifically with children and families impacted by family violence, I have found there are few services or programs that specialise in, or have taken advantage of, a father's desire to work directly on their relationship with their children over their relationship with their partner.

It may be assumed that repairing the relationship with their partner, being court ordered, or wanting future 'violence-free' adult relationships is the primary motivation for changing violent behaviours. This leaves untapped the enormous potential for wanting to learn how to be a better parent. The lack of programs for fathers who use violence is, I believe, tied to not wanting to exacerbate conflict due to the fear that this may put the infant or young child at further risk of harm. What terrifies me about this approach, however, is that literally thousands upon thousands of infants and children are still being left in the day-to-day care of fathers (and this extends to some mothers) who are violent, even if the other parent is protective. Worse still is when these same parents separate and their children are court ordered to attend access visits with a violent parent. Where there is a parent willing to work on bettering their parenting skills, and for the sake of their child, it is time we provided appropriate infant- and child-safe, skilled service responses to both mothers and fathers.

Capitalising on hope

In families where parents intuitively and proactively seek to understand and accommodate their newest family member, one's task as a worker is to fan a flame that already exists. In families which are clearly stuck, and with parents who are highly reactive and/or secretive and elusive, infants may hold the only key to entry. *This is not advocating an approach which uses the infant as the bait for hooking in the parent/s.* What I am suggesting is that infants and small children can represent hope for parents. This is in the form of repairing hurts from the past and creating something new. This is about capitalising on hope. Even when all hope seems to have departed, in the deepest, darkest recesses of the mind there exists the capacity to rekindle hope. German psychoanalyst and philosopher Erich Fromm in his 1968 book titled *The Revolution of Hope* wrote that:

> To hope means to be ready at every moment for that which is not yet born, and yet not become desperate if there is no birth in our lifetime. There is no sense in wishing for that which already exists or for that which cannot be. Those whose hope is weak settle down for comfort or for violence; those whose hope is strong see and cherish all signs of new life and are ready every moment to help the birth of that which is ready to be born. (Fromm 1968/2010, p.22)

He goes on further to state that 'as with every other human experience, words are insufficient to describe the experience. In fact, most of the time words do the opposite: they obscure it, dissect it, and kill it' (Fromm 1968/2010, p.24).

I find these sentiments highly evocative. They resonate with what I believe is the essence of infant-led work. This is the ability to recognise and excite what might be, and without a reliance on words. Infant work engages with that which lives within the emotional realm. Infant work lies in feeling comfortable with the non-verbal. It captures an essence of beginning and discovery. It is our job to excite what can be, and does so often, through how we bring attention to what the infant conveys about, and wants from, their relationship with their caregiver. Notwithstanding the reality that some parents do see their children as objects, or their property, or further bartering pieces in punishing or controlling their partners; all of us were once infants. The ability to think about our work with all adults, parents or not, benefits from a need to include those moments and times in life where we felt hopeful. These moments may feel hard to find.

Inter-generationally traumatised adults may often feel stuck. It is then effective to go back in time and discover what their hopes and dreams were. Take the time and persistence to explore who in their world either helped inspire them, or may have offered something, however large or small, towards them achieving their hopes and dreams. Revisiting times, places or aspects that held hope and reacquainting them with feelings of what could be helps with managing to deal with, rather than being crushed by, feelings of despair. Childhood is often at a period in life where, even amidst great familial deprivation, we may enjoy serendipitous and healing relational opportunities. This might perhaps be through certain friends, neighbours, teachers or extended family. While certain opportunities may have long passed, the feelings associated with these can be reawakened and used now, within their lives as adults, as parents, and within their relationship with their child.

Child-led approaches

The delineation between what is infant-led and what is child-led is somewhat artificial. For the child, it is a developmental progression accompanied by acquiring increasing verbal and cognitive skills which serves as the clearest marker. More than this, there operates a very powerful, and false, assumption that once a child begins to verbalise, they also begin to exist as a real person. The distinction for me is that as children acquire language and cognition, the range of activities available for engaging with and making meaning of certain events expands. We can, however, make assumptions about what works best with children and just how much or how little they understand, or can communicate. It might be beneficial to start from the position of not-knowing and coming to learn from the child themselves. Curiosity about and willingness to learn from and about the child offers the child who has had little experience of respectful interest from an adult a potentially powerful healing experience. Relating in this manner engages with the very core of what we all crave. This is to be considered worthy of becoming known, and valued for what we offer. Such relational experiences can then be tucked away, and stored with other relational treasures we may have collected along the way.

Be bold as every contact counts...
what has Faust got to do with it?

Fundamental to child- and infant-led practice is making 'every contact count'. Important neuro-physiological memories are being laid down in the infant and young child's developing brain and how we engage, or fail to engage, counts (Cozolino 2014). It is not the quantity so much as the quality of our engagement with children that leaves the deepest impression. High levels of transience or instability often prevent families from committing to long-term work. I may get only one contact or very limited contact with a child or family and I want that encounter to have a positive impact. My rule of thumb is not to expect the client/s to change to fit in with me, but consider how I might change my practice to fit in with them. Be bold, but not reckless, in working with infants and children. I have always loved a quote attributed to German playwright and philosopher, Johann Wolfgang von Goethe:

> Whatever you can do or dream you can, begin it.

> Boldness has genius, power and magic in it.

This quote is said to be from his famous play about Faust, and how he made a secret pact and sold his soul to the devil. The play itself, ironically, is full of relational violence and abuse, culminating in the drowning of an infant. The quote above, to my disappointment, is not an accurate translation of Goethe's words which read: 'Der Worte sind genug gewechselt, lasst mich auch endlich Taten sehn!'

(lines 214–215). Charles T. Brooks in 1856 offered this translation: 'Come, words enough you two have bandied, Now let us see some deeds at last…who hesitates will never be' (Goethe 1808). A German relative of mine provided me with more detail:

> It is a famous quote from Goethe's *Faust*, from the Prologue, in which the Theatre Director, the Poet and the 'funny person'/ the clown converse about what play should be performed. They are of different opinions. Finally, the Theatre Director finishes the conversation and somewhat impatiently urges his troupe on with these words: 'Der Worte sind genug gewechselt, lasst mich auch endlich Taten sehn'. 'The words are changed enough, also let me finally see deeds.' Or 'Enough words, actions finally too'. (Rechner 2016)

Ironically, I think these latter, more reliable translations, in addition to my becoming more familiar with Goethe's *Faust*, did even greater justice to the message I was trying to convey. This involves two points. First, it is not what is said, but how and what is done that matters for the infant. Infants need adults who will be congruent, be their advocates and be bold enough to ensure that they are included in the very matters that impact them most. Second, we (the adults) need to be available to see what children (infants especially) express about their world, and not collude with practices which keep violence secret, and therefore, not addressed. 'Enough words. Actions finally too.' We need to act when we see the possibilities of harm. We need to begin. This does not preclude forming therapeutic relationships or achieving therapeutic outcomes. This is the very point of this book. Beginning may involve the first step of bringing the subjective experience of the infant or young child into the consciousness of all concerned.

Acting for, and being led by the child is not simply about ensuring safety. We cannot afford to be hesitant when we may have limited chances to give meaning to the experience of children. When we are purposefully observant, we can find ample evidence of who they feel safest with, who they invite communication with, who they look at, look away from, if they ask for help or have learnt to manage alone (Chapter Five provides more detail regarding how very young children communicate). If we make it our practice consistently to involve children, engage with and be curious about them and make space for their perspective, sometimes, even in the most stuck families, magical things can happen. However, if we never involve them directly, nor bring them into our conversations with parents or consider their perspective, we remain adult centric. Being child-led is working from the belief that children are, and have the right to be, actively involved in the very issues that involve them. Child-led approaches are defined by engaging honestly with the child's feeling states. It involves our judgement, and our accountability, about how and when to do this safely. I will be so bold as to suggest that failing to truly bring the perspective of children into family violence work makes us complicit with actions which cause harm to children. By no means am I equating this with directly perpetrating harm. However, indirectly, by not recognising or asking for children's lived experience we may act as bystanders to actions which cause harm. Child-led and infant-led work simply affords children the same respect, responsiveness and attention we give to adults.

DEFINING FAMILY VIOLENCE

There is perhaps no perfect term to capture the complexity of relationships, nor intentions and behaviours that constitute fully the essence of what relational violence looks like (Hughes, Corbally & Kelowna 2014). In working within the area of family violence, I have developed a broad-brush acceptance that many configurations and presentations fit under this large umbrella term. Essentially 'family violence presupposes a relationship between those involved... Regardless of age, violence between family members is more common than violence between acquaintances or strangers' (Tolan, Gorman-Smith & Henry 2006, p.559). The term 'family violence' and its use in this book, retains the flexibility to cover all manner of abuses (including sexual) between adults and adults, adults and children, and children and children. It also presupposes that there is a blood and/or existing familial connection or relationship, and encompasses such terms as Intimate Partner Violence (IPV), Domestic Violence (DV) and Family Violence (FV). Most definitions refer to the use of coercion, control and aggression through physical, sexual, emotional, verbal and spiritual abuse, and which causes 'the family member to be fearful' (FCA 2013, p.4).

Gender and family violence

In my experience, working from an 'infant/child up', rather than an 'adult down' approach, challenges many of the common assumptions in the field of addressing family violence. Early in my career 1 was impressed with the work undertaken by Gail Ryan with young people and children who committed sex offences. Gail and her colleagues argued that in order to do effective work with children who commit sex offences, workers needed to retain their ability to remain empathic, while also holding young people and children to account (Ryan 1989; Ryan & Lane 1997). This included a capacity to make sense of what children do and why, and to make sense of the emotional disconnect involved in the capacity to reduce others to objects, whom they could then control and harm. This seemed to me to have application across all ages, gender and racial spectrums. As humans, we all possess the ability to hurt other humans. Coupled with this was what children directly taught me about how they saw the world.

My early work taught me, and my colleagues, that children would shut down if we talked in gendered stereotypes, and referred to men only as perpetrators, and women only as victims (Bunston 2002, 2008a; Bunston, Crean & Thomson-Salo 1999; Bunston & Heynatz 2006). This is not to say that these children (aged 8–12 years), were not themselves well versed with and already enacting gendered roles as young boys and young girls. However, when they spoke about their mum and their dad, they expressed varying degrees of affection, and fear, about both. As we began seeing their family members as people, not genders, they showed themselves as the complex, ambiguous, uncertain and confused young people they were. We involved male facilitators in our groups and even had a few fathers who participated in their own work alongside our mothers' groups. On occasion, we included fathers in our mothers' group where these fathers had also been the victims of violence. We also progressed to facilitating a group for fathers who had graduated from a men's behaviour change program, and their children (aged 3–13). More recently, we ran groups for fathers and their infants (Bunston 2001, 2008b, 2013b; Bunston & Heynatz 2006). Our infant work also taught us that we needed to include fathers and men in our thinking about our work. These infants either had an already established attachment to their fathers, or were likely to go on and develop one, in all its complexities, and needed a way for something good to come from this relationship (Jones & Bunston 2012).

I am not arguing against the vast research undertaken across the globe which identifies men as those who largely perpetrate violence against women and children (WHO 2009, 2013, 2014). I am, however, arguing that we are still a long way off acknowledging the violence of women against children and men and the violence which occurs in same-sex relationships, and of finding better ways to bring parents together to raise infants and children who are loved and cared for. If we get in early, and learn from infants and children, they might teach us something about how to raise better parents.

SUMMARY

Society today is awash with problems resulting in family violence. To reach dry land, we need new ways to respond to family violence. Currently, adult centric thinking dominates this landscape, largely discounting just how much infants and small children are impacted. Infant- and child-led approaches see the youngest members of the family as the most open and responsive to change. Additionally, they are fully able to participate as well as to communicate their experiences of family violence. Infants and small children most often carry hope for a different future, and in all things deserve to feel safe, and to be kept safe.

Chapter Two

Many took comfort in the belief that the infant neither remembered, nor was significantly impacted, by exposure to family violence. Now science has demonstrated, beyond any reasonable doubt, that this is not true. Infants not only carry physiological, unconscious memories of early relational trauma, but these relational experiences shape the subsequent development of their brain. There is no place for the infant, or for us, to hide from this painful truth.

Early Brain Development and the Emerging Self

There can surely be few working with infants and young children today who would not know something of the widely available and ever growing research into brain development. Most will have attended training, read articles or searched the internet to find the latest on what experts are telling us about the brain. Interest in the brain has gone viral! The US Congress declared the 1990s as the 'decade of the brain' (Cacioppo & Berntson 1992). Not surprisingly, this research primarily focused on the adult brain, and not on what was working, but what was not (Schore 2001a). Researchers became interested in understanding why some people developed severe mental health problems while others did not. The notion that adverse events occurring in early life need not define you should you access the right therapeutic treatment, and/or possess a resilient disposition, was being challenged. As one such researcher put it:

> Childhood maltreatment was understood either to foster the development of intra-psychic defence mechanisms that proved to be self-defeating in adulthood or to arrest psychosocial development, leaving a 'wounded child' within. Researchers thought of the damage as basically a soft-ware problem amenable

to reprogramming via therapy or simply erasable through the exhortation 'Get over it'. (Teicher 2002, p.68)

This quote suggests that people believed damage caused by psychological trauma experienced during childhood could be addressed through therapy or self-discipline. Brain science now demonstrates that we do not simply 'get over it'. Trauma, abuse and neglect inhibit the natural expansion of neural pathways which are forming within the infant's rapidly developing brain, and do cause damage (Schore 2016). 'To what degree and in what way' (Schechter & Willheim 2009, p.197) is the question which remains.

Imagine yourself as a baby born into a home where there is violence. This may be an experience some readers do not have to imagine. There may be occasions where one parent/caregiver protects or limits the impacts of the violence on the infant. When that adult is then under direct attack it may be neither safe nor possible to shield the infant. Unprotected, the developing infant simply cannot adequately protect themselves, and all their growing capacities will be directed towards survival. This can, depending on their age, physical and emotional development, involve them physiologically collapsing (dissociation), shutting down (freezing), becoming hypervigilant (fleeing), displaying excessive aggression (fighting) or, as they grow, using risk-taking behaviours. The younger the child, the less internal capacities they have at their disposal and the more likely they will be to dissociate. All of these defences serve to anaesthetise feelings of fear. In addition to managing their own distress, they witness terrifying behaviours between their caregivers. These are the very adults they instinctively gravitate towards when they are scared. As these traumatic experiences are repeated, the use of imperfect defence responses becomes entrenched (Perry 1997). This is despite such responses failing to alleviate their distress. In fact, the repeated use of such strategies for coping can and often does lead to other, increased relational problems which serve to distress them further (Perry *et al.* 1995). As the still immature child begins to enter the wider social world, these habitual responses fail to keep them safe. The anxiety and fear of living with such early trauma risks spilling over into all the child's other social interactions. A child can arrive at child care, kindergarten or school still in 'recovery mode' from the conflict which occurred the night before, and face the dread of returning home to the very place where more fearful events may yet come.

Further still, why would the same young child not expect violence to be present in any other setting, until proven otherwise? Day care, kindergarten and primary school are busy bustling places. Very little needs to happen for the child exposed to ongoing trauma to over-read cues in other settings and judge them as unsafe, even when they are not. Past experiences have shaped their expectations. These young children are primed and at the ready for anything even closely resembling their experiences of conflict at home, and rapidly triggered to defend themselves. As the traumatised young child faces the normal challenges of everyday life, their already depleted reserves can often prove woefully inadequate. They may not have a caregiver at home who can help them make sense of the events that occurred throughout their school day, let alone what happens at home. Despite the increased social isolation and emotional distress such behavioural responses typically create for the child, they do not know what else to do. This is the 'catch-22', self-defeating cycle these children may find themselves in. When required to defend themselves in infancy, primitive strategies for survival need to be utilised, and consolidated over time. How the child learns to protect themselves during infancy, no matter how fragile or futile this may have been, remains a powerful unconscious body memory that overrides our later-forming conscious, cognitive and verbal abilities (Rothschild 2000; Van der Kolk 2014).

A significant proportion of the family violence which impacts infants occurs even before birth (Chhabra 2007; Menezes-Cooper 2013). The baby in the womb is impacted by violence directly, (through the mother being physically assaulted) and/or indirectly by the presence of circumstances which create extreme and persistent levels of stress in the expectant mother. These stress hormones become part of the waters surrounding the baby. Similarly, the growing foetus can be affected by any alcohol or drugs the mother may use to 'cope' with the abuse and/or the secretion of powerful hormones in the womb, exposing the baby to overly high levels of cortisol (Quinlivan & Evans 2005; Talge, Neal & Glover 2007). This may result in the infant being at increased risk of developing neurodevelopmental difficulties, including hypervigilance, irritability and problems with concentration. So sensitive is the infant to their environment that even in 'so called' normal families, where moderate inter-parental conflict (raised voices only) occurs, the young baby has been found to be negatively affected (Graham, Fisher & Pfeifer 2013). As a worker 'on the ground' this is how I have made sense of this knowledge in my practice.

APPLYING THE SCIENCE

In this chapter I will share with you what I consider to be key information about neurobiology and the development of the brain, and theories that assist us to understand the world of the infant. The information I am sharing here is only the tip of the iceberg. If this book inspires you to find out more about infants and their mental and emotional wellbeing, then I have been successful in inviting you into this rich and exciting world of understanding: not just babies, but all of us, and the impact of our early lives has in shaping who we are and how we are in the world (see Appendix Two for suggested further reading in this area). I will explain what I have found to be the most useful ways of understanding these complex concepts and will offer case examples in this and subsequent chapters to illuminate their application within an infant- and child-led approach. The areas I will be covering are:

- the development of the brain
- the hierarchy of the brain
- what shuts down thinking
- how we match our internal world experiences with what we experience in our external world
- the power of our emotional self and the importance of mirror-neurons
- how the infant develops their sense of self
- why infant- and child-led work is 'right brain' work.

I will conclude with a summary of the key points in this chapter to prepare readers for the following chapter. This will be about outlining a working framework to guide your work with infants and children to bring about healing after violence.

Explaining the brain

The baby's brain begins its development during pregnancy but does not finish there. As Cozolino (2014) explains, the circumference of the infant's head has not fully developed prior to birth as this would truly shatter the mother's cervix (yes, it could be even worse!). As the newborn baby's brain continues to grow, the baby and their growing brain are incredibly vulnerable to the social and emotional environment. The caregiving environment and these early family relationships directly affect how the infant's brain grows and what connections are made within and between the vast number of potential and possible neurological pathways. This is because the nature of emotional and social relating in early childhood leaves its own unique footprints which, when repeated, set up unique pathways of neural connections in the growing brain of each child, sculpted and shaped by their experience. The brain develops rapidly in these early stages and the actual brain box, or skull, itself does not cease growing until adolescence (Cozolino 2014).

The early stages of brain development set the foundation and are important (Perry 2005). They pre-date language development, and remain influential throughout our whole lives. They determine how we make sense of the world through how our body reads and interprets what is happening around us. However, while this part of the brain is the foundation from which all other growth emerges, it is seen to remain operational in our unconscious world (Schore 2016); that is, although it happens, we are not aware of it. Our body reads what is happening through what is known as the autonomic nervous system (Rothschild 2000), which determines our bodily functions. This manages things such as our heart rate, breathing, reflexes, bowel and bladder control and the pupils of our eyes. It inhabits the spinal system which is connected to the brain stem, with the brain operating as the largest component of our central nervous system and recognised as the control centre (Rothschild 2000). The more safe, consistent, loving and playful the experiences the infant has in their relationships with family members, the more solid, complex and rich will be the varying pathways from this primitive (i.e., first) unconscious brain. This will influence everything that follows, through to the more advanced, conscious brain which includes curiosity and the capacity to think and to learn.

With enough positive caregiving experiences, over time a child's skill grows in language development, problem solving, social and emotional mastery. The infant's capacities become more sophisticated as they develop over time, should they have what Winnicott (1960) called 'good enough' relational experiences, rather than 'perfect' ones, which are neither possible nor desirable. The ability for operating in what is called the 'higher order' levels of functioning in the brain develops. Higher order functioning enables our capacity to be empathic and insightful, to be imaginative, to learn from our past mistakes, to seek out and ask for help when we need it and to give help to others in need. It also, very importantly, helps us in grow our capacity and ability to form healthy and robust friendships and other relationships, and to manage emotionally challenging and painful events (Perry 2005; Perry *et al.* 1995; Perry & Szalavitz 2006). It has been argued that what enabled humans (in comparison to other species) to evolve the capacity for speech and higher order brain functioning was the power of the mother–infant bond for survival (MacLean 1982). For all mammals, including humans, the group of animals that no longer hunt for food to feed their young, but who produce milk for their babies, the newborn's survival is dependent upon the relationship with, and connection to, their mother. This relationship is imperative for survival and 'the young's separation cry that enables the mother to locate her lost offspring might have been one of the first examples of mammalian vocalization' (Lambert 2003, p.346). It was this instinct to protect the infant and remain relationally engaged which is believed by some to have led to the eventual development of our human brain, which is more complex in evolutionary terms than other mammalian brains because of its developed complex outer/higher layer called the neocortex. This evolutionary development of higher order functioning in the human brain is not a statement of value, but of explaining how the structure of our brain differs, and has built a structure of what comes before, and sets the foundation, or building blocks, for all our subsequent development.

Three brains for the price of one – the triune brain

Paul D. MacLean made an important contribution to our understanding of the brain (Newman & Harris 2009). His research was concerned with how the human brain evolved and its emotional functioning. He maintained that, as with all species, humans have evolved over time and so too has our brain. In prehistoric times, the first humans' brains operated necessarily simply in survival mode. When our more primitive ancestors sensed danger, they reacted to stay alive. Over hundreds of thousands of years we have progressed from what MacLean (1990) called the 'proto-reptilian brain' (reactive and primitive), to the 'paleo-mammalian' brain (emotional, with capacity for learning and memory), to the 'neo-mammal' or 'human brain' (conscious with capacity for vocalisation and empathy). It is not a simple replacement of one with the other, but a process of building one upon the other. So essentially we now have three different brain domains that operate as one and that are inter-dependent, in both structure and function. MacLean (1982) explained that we have retained 'the features of three basic evolutionary formations that reflect an ancestral relationship with reptiles, early mammal and recent mammals... the three formations form a hierarchy of three brains in one – a triune brain' (p.291). MacLean's theory about the brain is not without its critics because, as with most research and the theories it generates, perhaps especially in understanding the brain, each new hypothesis or theory is one interpretation (Cory 2002). I have found this explanation very helpful in my work.

The first domains are described as our lower brain (or brain stem), and the second or mid brain (or limbic system). Both of these regions or domains are connected to our emotional, non-verbal (and youngest and earliest) self. MacLean identified that our emotional self, embedded in these low to mid brain regions, is closely linked to what is known about Broca's area. This area, (discovered by Paul Broca in the later 1800s) is responsible for speech and operates as a connection point between the lower and mid brain regions (Newman & Harris 2009).

This knowledge helped me make sense of why so many of the young children I have worked with appear to have language delays. If an infant experiences trauma, this takes place before language and a capacity for reasoning are developed. This means that early trauma not only cannot be spoken about, but the traumatic experiences themselves rob the infant of the dependable, calm, relationship experiences necessary for boosting the development of growth of these critical areas of brain architecture and function.

Further still, it is important to know that, at the age, trauma which threatens our survival triggers our non-verbal response, immediately activating the body's regulatory systems. Van der Kolk (2014) writes 'trauma by nature drives us to the edge of comprehension, cutting us off from language based experience or even an imaginable past' (p.43). Understanding how the brain handles trauma makes sense of why soldiers and civilians exposed to the horrors of war find it hard not only to forget the horrendous things they have witnessed but also struggle to give words to them. If adults struggle to give words to the feeling states they experience in relation to suffering they have endured as adults, imagine how much more the still-developing child will struggle with giving verbal expression to or even understanding their emotional states when the brain structure and function necessary to develop these abilities are being disrupted and interrupted as they form.

MacLean's research suggests that the primitive or reptilian brain or brain stem is the first and most dominant brain region (Cozolino 2008). Although it takes less than a split second, feelings come first, and thinking comes later. No matter how considered and thoughtful we believe we are, all of us interpret the world first through our feeling states before we are able to think about our experience.

Instinctively, we are inclined to give our feelings greater authority than our reasoning, unless we have developed our capacity to do otherwise. Our later-developing reasoning abilities can be just as powerful, but need to be nurtured in early life and continually developed throughout life. Our ability to reflect, engage in problem solving and sophistication in thinking is involved in what constitutes the third (and specific to the human) brain. This sits on top of the lower two. This third brain holds the capacity for much greater complexity in thought, reflection, abstract learning and emotional regulation. This last function refers to the ability to reflectively think about, judge and manage or choose our actions and reactions, rather than be managed or controlled by our feeling states.

Unable to think! Short-circuiting the brain

How does this knowledge then inform our practice with very small children and their parents impacted by family violence? Where the experience of violence in relationships has been inter-generational, it is not simply the child who is struggling with emotional expression but often their parents as well. MacLean's work (MacLean 1982, 1990), and that of others, such as Bruce Perry (Perry 1997, 2005; Perry *et al.* 1995) and Allan Schore (Schore 2001b, 2003a), indicate that the person who has been highly traumatised from a very young age is less likely to have well-developed access to their higher order brain functioning. This is not about who is, or is not, smart. Higher order functioning is about being able to manage and reflect on one's feeling states. This involves possessing wisdom or insight, and the capacity to critically reflect on and examine what you are feeling and why. When you have developed this capacity, rather than rushing to judgement about yourself or others, you can tolerate powerful feelings and think about what they might mean.

Needing to survive family violence from a very young age generates an excessive reliance on needing to monitor any potentially dangerous feeling states. What can be sacrificed is a freedom within which to play, discover, imagine and explore, in companionship with, and under the loving gaze of, a caregiver. These developmental opportunities are critical to healthy development (Stern 2003; Trevarthen 2001). These form the stepping stones needed to build the pathways which allow access across and up to the many different facets of our experience, personality, beliefs, memories, skills and capabilities. Being 'on guard' constantly robs us of the opportunity to build these steps to discovery. The priority is instead to bunker down, or as Rifkin-Graboi *et al.* (2009) explain, the infant exposed to acute stress is preoccupied with 'shunting the majority of his or her energy to the areas of the body and the brain that will aid in immediate survival' (p.63). The ongoing nature of family violence can establish a constant readiness for incoming fire. They need to build themselves an internal bunker, where other little ones who feel safe are free to play, enjoy and be enjoyed. The child living with family violence may be too busy, and may in fact be exhausted by the demands of simply keeping safe. Constant exposure to trauma from an early age increases their sensitivity to what is perceived to be potential danger rather than what might always be real danger. The filter between feeling and thinking has had little support to develop. Reacting overrides reflecting, particularly when a sense of fear or anxiety is triggered. This leads to what I have described as a sort of 'short-circuiting' process, where functioning remains reactive, in the lower brain, and unable to ascend to reflection, in higher level brain functioning.

The small child who has experienced family violence hears screaming in the playground and may be instantly transported back to their body memory of fear. Their survival mechanisms kick in. These survival mechanisms live in the oldest and most primitive emotional domain of the lower levels of the brain. Should they not be able to see, recognise, or have another person help them understand that the screams are attached to non-threatening interactions, they may need to remain in that primitive state. Their reactive 'reptilian brain' fires up, and their higher order thinking brain dampens down. The small child who has not experienced ongoing exposure to relational violence or conflict may, or may not, be alarmed by the scream but can assess their emotional state by accessing their higher order 'human' brain and can think about and/or be available to investigate other explanations for the screaming. The screaming may evoke a very different bodily recall for this child such as excitement, laughter or play. This child who has not been exposed to family violence is more likely to mentally explore the possibilities of, and make a more considered judgement about, the meaning of the screaming.

Where there is no safe and/or reflective relationship to help, the child makes their own sense of the world, and potentially problematic thinking related to highly reactive emotional states becomes more fixed, and harder to shift, the older they become. Adults with unprocessed early childhood and subsequently occurring traumas may become somewhat black and white in their thinking, and very quick to judge. Meeting a professional worker, or school counsellor, or family support worker, can immediately raise their hackles. When one has lived much of their life operating from the reptilian (lower) brain, they can perceive threat as coming from anywhere (Cozolino 2008). This means that any perceived threat quickly surfaces, for example, 'Are you going to take my children from me?' 'Do you think I am a bad parent?

Will you tell on me to social services?' Workers may be seen less as a 'real' person and more as a 'cut-out character', a reminder of how authority figures have deceived them, or worse still, abused them in the past. Younger children, if they perceive or imagine danger may also quickly move to their reptilian brain, and react. The trigger for this may be obvious or impossible to fathom, by others or themselves. A smell, colour, noise, word or action has snapped them into action. Their teacher, worker or fellow student, who only moments before was their friend has suddenly morphed into a dragon and they need to flee, brandish their sword or wrap themselves in their invisibility cloak (courtesy of J.K. Rowling's Harry Potter).

The development of the 'emotional' right brain

A prominent researcher into brain development, Allan Schore, suggests that the right side of our brain develops first, and does so within the first couple of years of life. The left brain then becomes the more dominate focus in growth for a period of a few years, then for slow periods of time this pattern moves back and forth, integrating the functioning between both hemispheres until early adulthood (Schore 2001b, 2003a, 2003b, 2016). In this beginning period, our right brain is imprinted with what are known as early implicit memories. These memories are hidden away in our unconscious world where they remain, stored in the memory bank of our body. Our right brain is sometimes described as our emotional brain, and within the initial period of right brain growth, the infant, together with their caregiver, begins the job of developing 'affect regulation' skills. This is the capacity to manage the feelings that accompany our more basic needs, such as being hungry, tired, cold, overexcited or unwell. As the caregiver assists the dependent infant to manage the emotions connected to their physical experience of their body, the infant, ideally, also takes in the love, nourishment, enjoyment and care. This leaves physical memories of how they move from a distressed state (I need it 'now') into a more 'regulated' or managed (Ah! that's better) state. Over time, with 'good enough', not perfect, caregiving, the infant can develop, at this initially implicit (embedded) memory level, the capabilities to soothe themselves and trust that in time, their needs will be safely met. By the time the young child has begun schooling, and where they have received 'good enough' caregiving, they possess capacity to manage their own emotional states most of the time (Rifkin-Graboi *et al.* 2009).

Consistent with a 'short-circuiting process' that can operate in the hierarchy of the 'triune' (three levels of) brain, what is important to know is that these early emotional and social experiences develop before the capacity for language develops. When one's early experiences are 'good enough', and the left brain's growth spurt begins following our second year of life, language skills proceed to develop, largely free of any major obstacles. The left brain hemisphere is considered to manage our verbal skills, and our pragmatic, thinking self. However, the two sides need to work in tandem. One such connection point is a bridge known as the 'corpus callosum'. Unfortunately, the capacity of this bridge to enable movement between both the emotional (right) and the thinking (left) brain has been shown to be significantly reduced by exposure to early childhood abuse and maltreatment (including exposure to violence) of any kind (Teicher 2002; Teicher *et al.* 2003, 2004). What this means is that the integration between feelings and the capacity to make sense of these feelings is compromised. As mentioned already, the energy taken to survive early childhood trauma gets in the way of giving the emotional right brain the best start in life. When growth in the left brain takes off, the young child is already 'behind the game'.

Inside out and outside in

Aside from fighting for survival and the resulting excessive sensitivity to potential dangers, when an infant or child experiences early trauma, there is a failure in the experience of congruence. Congruence refers to a matching, or actual, correspondence between what the infant learns about what they feel inside and how it matches with their outside experience, and vice-versa (Bürgin 2011). For example, the parent who shushes their toddler and tells them everything is fine when their partner is smashing up the room is trying, perhaps, to be protective and possibly minimise the likelihood of the infant attracting harmful attention. As the child moves into survival mode, the levels of adrenaline (or endogenous epinephrine) start pumping and heighten the body's memory of this experience (Van der Kolk 2014). They may be processing overwhelming feelings of fear on the inside, with messages from their protective parent about their external world that do not match. Not only is their inside world telling them 'this is terrifying' while their parent is saying, 'no, it's ok', their internal world may be wanting to scream, to run, to smack, but their body may shut down completely and freeze on the spot.

The infant is left traumatised, not seeing any consistency in actions, feelings or words. Not having anyone to help them manage or make sense of something that, for most, makes little sense. When this incongruence is coming from their parents or caregivers, in the infant's home, and where violence is unlikely to occur 24 hours a day, nor maybe even weekly, there may also be moments of tenderness, laughter or companionship and cooperation. The good stuff recedes quickly, however, when the bad stuff threatens, and is slow to return even when the storm has passed. Even the good stuff can seem to make little sense for a child, as how can one day be filled with happy memories, and then the next so bad that the happy memories feel like a lie?

Building a light to pierce the night sky – using our emotional self

Do not under-estimate how important you as a worker can be, or how healing the relationships are that we offer. Imagine being outside in the dark of night. There are no stars and in every direction, all you see is black. Then one lone light pierces the night sky. It is a lighthouse far off in the distance. Where do your eyes turn? You look towards the light because this shaft of light cuts through the darkness. As workers, foster carers or other caregiving adults, our contact with infants, children and families can be so different from what has been experienced before that we stand out. We can offer an emotional honesty to infants and small children which speaks to their hunger to be truly be seen by someone, and reflect this back to them in a congruent way (Morgan 2007). We can often try to help children who seem sad to feel better. Sitting alongside an infant, and being open to feeling their sadness, depression or fear, is congruent and offers them recognition of their feeling states, companionship and comfort. It is enormously powerful when you give back, through words, the tone of your voice, and/or your emotional expression, validation about what they are feeling through what they are expressing. You may not get it exactly right, but the intention to do so is there, and may be experienced by the infant as such. This works when we are truly allowing ourselves to be open to feeling what the infant or very young child is telling us. As argued by Reddy & Trevarthen (2004), 'if we want to know what a baby, an adult or, indeed, any animal feels or thinks, we have to engage with them, allowing ourselves to feel the sympathetic response that the other's actions and feelings invite' (p.9).

Engaging with the feelings of a distressed infant or young child is truly painful for workers and carers. This may be why we sometimes collude with adult centric practices. We see our jobs as hard enough, without having to take home the 'felt' memory of a frightened or emotionally hungry infant or small child we worked with that day. For the worker, foster or kinship carer, this is particularly so when we feel uncertain about the quality of the caregiving environment the infant or child will return to. The reciprocity of this work offers us an amazing privilege, and as much as we carry distressing memories of certain infants and children we have met, we also find ourselves witness to and participants in astounding moments of beautiful engagement, relational shifts and rapid recovery. Further to this, can we leave an infant or small child alone to shoulder such crushing distress? Foster and/or kinship carers are amongst those who offer front-line recovery work when and if the removal of a child is deemed necessary. But this is not the only time this can be done, and neither are they the only workers who can do this. The opportunities to engage compassionately, and fully, with an infant or child may occur only briefly or may be ongoing.

As I stated in Chapter One, every contact counts. And as a collective of carers and professionals involved in the lives of the very young, together we can help illuminate the way. We do this in one way by offering the infant an experience of what it feels like to be seen, and thought about (Thomson-Salo 2007). This involves a process of introspection, or 'mentalisation' where we develop an awareness of how we may come across to others as well as an appreciation of what might be occurring for another. 'Children learn to mentalise by being mentalised, that is, when others have their mind in mind' (Allen, Fonagy & Bateman 2008, p.316).

Mirror, mirror on the wall

It is believed that mirror-neurons are involved in this 'mind to mind connection'. They occupy a specific area in the brain (the premotor cortex which sits within the frontal lobes) and are believed to tie together our sense of self and sense of other (Uddin *et al.* 2007). This area of the brain has been responsible for 'aspects of the mind, such as empathy, imitation, synchrony, and even the development of language' (Van der Kolk 2014, p.58). Mirror-neurons exist from birth and are engaged through our relationships with others. One way of understanding how our own mirror-neurons work is to consider how we feel about working with certain clients. Time to be truthful now. We all have, or have had, families who we struggle in working with. This may be because deep down we are frightened of them, we may resent them, not respect or even like them. It is not unusual with such families for us to sometimes make excuses about not being available to take their phone calls, or meet their demands, particularly when they are frequent, and no matter what we do, we never seem to stem the tide of their wants and demands.

When we sit with families or individuals who are reactive, crisis driven, overly demanding or hostile, we are triggered to defend ourselves. We, too, as mature and as wonderful as we are, are likely, at times, to mirror their behaviour. We too can bunker down, and react defensively, operating from our lower brain, and not quite thinking through our reactions, and actions. We can find ourselves mirroring the reactivity of our clients, keen to make a quick exit, rather than to sit with the enormity of the painful and angry feelings they may be evoking in us. We may become 'out of synch'. Our usual, thoughtful, compassionate selves disappear, and we risk becoming 'in synch' with their 'bunker down', 'trust no one' and 'don't let anyone in' state of mind (see Chapter Three, and Diagram 1 'Hierarchy of Brain Functioning and Triggering Emotional Reactions in Others', p.59). What is significant about realising that we can mirror our clients is the recognition that our clients can mirror us! There are many things we can do to 'keep mentalising' (or thinking reflectively) and some of how this is done 'in the moment' will be described in the following chapters, and particularly in the explanation of the importance of 'reflective supervision' (see Chapter Eight).

Developing a robust sense of self

Infants possess their own separate experiences. Research demonstrates that even in the earliest stages infants possess moments of what Stern (2003) calls 'primary consciousness'. This involves a gradual unfolding of a 'self', which emerges through how they organise their physical and sensory world (what sounds they hear, how they experience the touch of others, smells they are exposed to, and sights they see). These are taken in through their body and senses and occur fundamentally within the context of their relationship experiences, creating certain patterns which cluster together as the beginning of some sort of meaning for the infant as they develop.

Critical to 'infant- and child-led' practice is the knowledge that the small child is their own unique person, who has reactions and experiences in conjunction with their carers, but which are distinct from them as well. To achieve a healthy sense of self, the infant, who from the very beginning of life possesses a core-self, moves to developing a domain of core-relatedness (two to six months of age), and starts to recognise that their mother, or main caregiver, is separate from themselves. This leads to 'secondary inter-subjectivity' (Stern 2003). 'Inter-subjectivity' occurs throughout life, through the meanings we make about ourselves, and about others, and through how we relate to one another. 'These processes of self and interactive regulation are simultaneous, complementary, and optimally in dynamic balance, with flexibility to move back and forth' (Beebe & Lachmann 1998, p.481). The infant, when they reach approximately nine months, can match or read, as well as misread, the mental states of others depending on the steadiness and quality of the caregiving relationship (Stern 2003). Stern also recognised that these timelines were somewhat artificial, as ongoing research continues to extend the boundaries of what we think we know about the interpersonal world of the infant.

Using our right brain to inform our left brain and our left brain to manage our right

When we can recognise and reflect on our own feeling states, together with those we work with, and not just simply react, we are accessing our higher order brain functioning. This is what enables us to consider different vantage points. It's like looking at the outside of a building and its surrounds, while simultaneously exploring what's inside the building. We can begin to evaluate this swirl of feelings and wonder about what they might be telling us about ourselves and our clients. We can take a questioning view, or 'meta-perspective', and we can recognise what our emotions are telling us, without having to react to them. In fact, staying with our emotional self is critical to infant and child work, as this is the domain they largely operate in. They are communicating with us through emotions and behaviours, and it is this non-verbal world that we want to access and understand.

Rather than being frightened of what the vulnerable infant or the difficult family triggers in us, we can befriend our emotions, and theirs, and begin to listen to the story they might be telling us. We can ask ourselves, 'what feelings sit underneath the behaviours I am being presented with?' and, 'what might these tell me about the vulnerabilities they are trying to manage?' 'Does the client I find hard to like, not like himself very much?' 'Might they have felt this from their caregivers, and now expect it from all others?' 'Does the baby who will not return my gaze, turn away because it is frightening to look into the faces of others, or, might he feel confused when he finds his carer's face unresponsive, and expect the same from mine?' Using our mind to try and understand their mind may have the impact of infants, children and adults experiencing us in a very different manner. We might offer the contrast to their dark sky; remaining able to mentalise in the face of overwhelming feelings, and not simply mirroring back what they most fear – an ugly reflection of themselves. Understanding, with empathy, the sometimes unhelpful behaviours our clients may have learnt to defend themselves, can powerfully shift our feelings. When we move from being reactive, to genuinely wanting to make sense of their world, we might just find they become available to mirror what they see and feel coming from us: someone wanting to befriend, and not harm them.

Theories that help healing

As helping professionals, we are often so much better at identifying what is wrong with others than what to actually do to help heal them. This is perhaps because as humans, though similar in so many ways, we are also incredibly diverse. We have a sense of what are helpful approaches when working with others. These include building on the strengths of others, consolidating what has worked previously, and challenging thoughts or beliefs that are counter-productive. These approaches tend to be more successful with those who have had one or more people in their lives who have been available to them in times of real need. Some people who have experienced significant, ongoing trauma may have not had any noteworthy support. Infants and small children tend to be the most receptive to engaging with others, and have been described as 'hard wired' to connect (Siegel 2001). In fact, the neuroplasticity of the brain in these formative stages allows for remarkable opportunities for neural repair to occur, particularly in the first 12 months (Shatz 1992). Infants and children often provide the starting point, allowing workers into families that may be otherwise difficult to engage. However, in some circumstances, these infants and children have been removed, and live with extended family or foster carers, who may find the behaviours of their new 'foster' children both difficult to understand, or manage. As the following chapters will outline, there are many things we can do to bring about healing for such children and families. Before moving on, however, in conjunction with the infant- and child-led approach outlined in Chapter One, and the neurological and developmental aspects discussed in this chapter, the following descriptions outline some additional theories I have found invaluable in guiding my work.

Ghosts and angels in the nursery

This idea is taken from an article now regarded as a classic. Fraiberg, Adelson & Shapiro (1975) wrote about a small group of clients, who due to their own severe and early childhood abuse could not emotionally engage with their own babies. These mothers and fathers had bunkered down so much so, that they could not see, or feel, the distress of their own children, having built such thick defensive walls around themselves. The frightening ghosts of their own early childhood experiences got in the way of the present relationship with their babies. The work of Fraiberg and her colleagues, looked at helping these parents to feel compassion for themselves as children, as well as to feel safe enough to revisit emotionally what they had spent years being too frightened to consider. This infant-focused work, through supporting the parent to feel their own vulnerabilities, assisted them to see the vulnerabilities felt by their infants. Thirty years later Lieberman and colleagues (2005) published their article which extended this work, introducing the notion of angels in the nursery. This looked at finding those positive moments, or experiences of being cared for, that could be passed on, and built upon, in their relationship with their own infants and children.

Watch, wait, wonder

Developed as a means of encouraging parents to move to a more reflective space, this approach uses this simple mantra as a very effective way of reminding parents (and workers) to slow down, not to immediately react, and to wonder about what they see unfolding for the infant (Cohen 2006; Cohen *et al.* 1999; Muir, Lojkasek & Cohen 1999). This is something I have found incredibly useful to apply to my work, not only with infants and children, but with adults, groups, couples and families. Waiting, and watching, is not something as workers we often feel comfortable doing. We can rush about, trying to fix what we assume is the problem, rather than spending time simply being curious and wondering about what might be going on, not just through words, but actions, feelings, non-verbal communication and dynamics. Watching who a toddler goes to, or does not go to, in a group setting; how a mother manages her infant when she herself needs to use the toilet, does she take her infant, or leave her infant with you, does she tell the infant what she is doing, or simply disappear; how often does a mother bring her infant to her breast and use her breast as the 'go to' solution for all things, or does she try and find out what her infant wants? We can collect an enormous amount of information to play with in our minds, or, with the infants, children and adults, to wonder about aloud, and to try together to better understand.

Match, mismatch and repair

This is another very useful mantra that comes from the work of Ed Tronick. Videos of his research using the 'still face experiment' can be easy found on the internet. This research has found that for even the 'good enough' parent, there is usually a mismatch between what the infant wants and what the parent gives. This mismatch occurs approximately 70 per cent of the time. This means that only about 30 per cent of the time do the parent and infant, or young child, come together and match each other's feeling states accurately (Tronick 2007). The destination (matching each other) is not what is always most important. The important element of the relationship is the journey, where both try together to find out what is happening for the other. This mismatch and the repair process give both the opportunity for discovery in themselves and each other (i.e., when I do this my mother laughs; when I am hurt and cry, Mummy picks me up and I feel better and I am happy to play again). Together we find a solution that works well enough for each of us. This is a powerful encouragement to offer parents where the success rate for matching their infant or child's feeling states would, in many instances, be significantly less than 30 per cent. What this research, and the concept of 'match, mismatch and repair' offers, is an acknowledgment that no parent gets it right 100 per cent of the time. For the parent who may already, deep down, consider themselves to be an unlovable or bad parent, this presents an opportunity for repair. The goal here is not to always get it right, whatever that may look like, but to try and figure out what might be happening for their child. This shifts black and white thinking to an unknown colour, as the object is not right or wrong but somewhere in between.

Attachment theory

The most well-known and widely applied theory to help us understand the relational world of infants and children is attachment theory. Categories of attachment are used to describe the relationships we form as infants with our caregivers, and how these remain in play throughout our lives. Today there is an enormous emphasis on attachment theory, the neurological implications of early childhood caregiving relationships, and how these shape the development of the brain (Bretherton 1991; Jaremka et al. 2013; Luijk et al. 2011; Schore 2005; Schore & Schore 2008; Siegel 2012). The foundational work of psychiatrist John Bowlby and psychologist Mary Salter in the 1950s explored how the quality of the infant's relational security impacted their development (Salter-Ainsworth & Bowlby 1991). This work was further extended by Mary Main and her colleagues as they then researched how early relationship experiences played out in adult relationships (Main & Hesse 1990; Main, Kaplan & Cassidy 1985; Main & Solomon 1990).

Attachment is seen largely as a behavioural system motivated by the goal of finding security for ourselves through our relationships with others. It is what can be observed in the infant (crying, gazing, vocalising and movement) that gives us clues about what is being felt. This 'attachment behaviour system' is activated by threat, distress and/or separation from an attachment figure, as well as being in new situations. How the attachment (caregiving) figure responds when these behaviours are activated is seen to directly impact on the infant's developing attachment or relating style (Crowell & Treboux 2006). 'Representations' or 'working models' of attachment refer to a dynamic that organises our pattern of relating to others. An adult's individual attachment style is understood to derive from their early childhood attachment experience, which acts as a 'model' for later intimate relationships. It is believed these models of relating can be handed down from generation to generation (Crowell & Treboux 2006).

Roughly, there are two styles, or categories of attachment, *secure* and *insecure*. An individual operating from a *secure* working model of attachment exhibits a robustness and confidence in exploring their environment, both externally and, as they mature, internally, as they experience safety in the knowledge that loved ones will remain available to support, guide and nurture them. An *insecure* working model arises when the caregiver's behaviour creates, rather than reduces, anxiety in the infant. Even in the face of unpredictable, rejecting and possibly harmful responses, the infant will tend to remain connected to their caregiver. This can lead to internalising, or the organising, of working models of attachment that involve coping strategies of *avoidance* or *ambivalence* (Main 1991). An *insecure avoidant* strategy involves the infant minimising the need for contact. This is to avoid painful feelings of rejection, while at the same time remaining watchful and aware of their caregiver, even if from a distance. Feelings of neediness are minimised and pushed off into the unconscious. Conversely, an *insecure ambivalent* strategy, involves the infant maximising contact with an inconsistent caregiver, but showing submissive behaviours or even a reversal of roles where they take on the care of the caregiver.

The third insecure strategy identified by Mary Main, is *disorganised*, and appears to be less common in the general population and emerged as a third, discrete classification as a result of ongoing research into children's attachment behaviours (Main 1991; Salter-Ainsworth & Eichberg 1991). This strategy demonstrates more severe and chaotic coping mechanisms. They include bizarre and confused responses as well as 'freezing' or rigid movements (Holmes 1993). This category involves the infant failing to find a strategy with which to cope with attachment related stress (Main 1991). This relational response, from my experience, is not uncommon in the infants and children who live with ongoing and severe family violence.

SUMMARY

The infant's rapidly developing brain is shaped by their early caregiving relationship experiences. These experiences impact on how well the growing child learns to manage their emotional reactions, and directly contribute to how well they develop their capacity to be self-reflective and self-aware. Being aware of the three levels of brain functioning can help us understand how the infant brain and sense of self develop. Where early, ongoing trauma is present, a 'short-circuiting' can occur which serves as an important survival mechanism, but which, over time, can result in the growing child remaining stuck in unhelpful lower brain responses. Importantly, recognising that our sense of self develops within the context of relating to others, makes it imperative that, as workers, we reflectively engage with our own emotional states when we work with infants and young children. We can and will make a powerful difference if we see, honour and respond honestly to the infant's experience. This begins with our ability to see and respond honestly to our own.

Chapter Three

We offer infants and children healing not by what we do to them but by how we are with them. We see them, hear them and respond to them, both as separate to their primary caregiver and, simultaneously, within the context of their relationship with their caregiver. The violence they have experienced in relationships is real. So too are their emotional responses. Therefore, the relationship we offer must also be authentic. Healing involves respecting how they need to be to survive, and seeing beyond this, to how they may be if supported to thrive.

Developing Models of Thinking and Practice

This is a book about infants and small children who, through no fault of their own, have been exposed to what most would consider overwhelming challenges. It is also about how we, as adults (workers, foster/kinship carers, extended family members) relating with infants and children impacted by family violence can seek to access the part of them which has needed to remain hidden in order to survive, and thereby increase their capacity to flourish. We can offer children and their parents relationships which can heal by engaging with them genuinely and by seeking to understand them and what they have needed to do to survive. This includes being interested in them and their experience and finding value in them. This chapter is about what we, the adults (workers, carers, etc), can do differently, not the child. It is also about not 'giving up' on these children and their families, even when they are challenging, difficult to engage, ambivalent about us and not easy, able or likeable. Understanding and being sensitive to the meaning made of early traumatic events which may have robbed them of relationships in which they were able to feel safe and valued is crucial, and explored further in the next chapter.

In the first two chapters of this book, I explained what infant- and child-led approaches are, as well as to presenting research and theories which explain how relationships where there are issues such as family violence harm young ones, and how other relationships can heal. Without offering ready-made answers, this chapter brings together some practical ways to think about how we might go about working with infants, children and their caregivers impacted by family violence. It starts with us, and how we work, think and then act. It involves discovering the answer to the most important question raised by this book: *how do I practise in a way that makes explicit my commitment to infant- and child-led practice?*

There are no ready-made solutions. As workers or even carers, we tend to think in terms of what we get our clients, or the children we care for, doing. The idea of picking up a resource that says 'here is the answer, this is what you do', or 'just follow these steps and you will get these results' may work for children and families with uncomplicated lives, but even then I really doubt that. We are human beings, we are complex and we respond in vastly different ways to different stimuli, situations and people. My experience is that the most successful approach is based on respectful, real relationships. For most people, that involves someone else demonstrating that they are interested in them and their experience, and that they strive to understand, as much as they can, what they have been through. This 'striving to understand' is what can lead us to seeing others differently. 'Seeing others differently' can lead us to relating to others differently. What we bring into the relationship is as important as respecting what is brought into the relationship by others and the notion of reciprocity: the back and forth exchange in relating. A model for 'thinking emotions' (our own and others) will be presented and then some suggested guiding practice principles. The ideas I am presenting aim to counter early, sometimes unconscious, life experiences where infants, children and adults have struggled to feel seen or thought about.

A MODEL FOR 'THINKING EMOTIONS'

The diagram below illustrates how we can help ourselves become conscious of what we are feeling to help us think about others, particularly during highly charged, distressing or overwhelming situations. It offers a visual reminder of how we can unconsciously mirror the feeling states of the infants and children we work with, as well as their families. When those we are working with are operating from a lower order brain level, often to defend themselves from what was and is now perceived to be a threat, we too can find ourselves becoming reactive, distressed and unable to reflect on what is happening right before us. How we are, and what we do in these situations can offer clients something different emotionally. This difference can cut through what is sometimes the emotionally reactive ricocheting we may experience with some clients. Not simply reacting back, but genuinely reflecting on what might be behind this child's (or parent's) oppositional behaviour, sullen appearance or agitation immediately feeds back an unexpected relational encounter. This chance, albeit sometimes seemingly small, may prompt them to also mirror back something new and different.

Case example: Nick (aged 11)

Nick was a young boy I worked with in a group for children who had experienced family violence. Physically he was the biggest boy in the group and quickly assumed the role of 'top dog'. In the group he was clearly relishing the power of this position. Perhaps as this was not something he felt inside. As one of the group facilitators, rather than engage in (and mirror) a tussle of 'who's the boss' with this young boy, it was much more effective for me to reflect on why he was so eager to enact the role of commando in the group. I had the sense that at home, and with his father, he felt very small, unprotected and powerless. Rather than overt this in front of the other boys, something that may have further exposed his sense of vulnerability, I responded to Nick as a young boy who felt powerless and, I suspected, often afraid. I began a game with Nick whenever he became overly boisterous or controlling of others. This involved me running after him with the threat that I would hug him. This response to his oppositional behaviour seemed to quickly deflate his need to puff himself up in the group, and he would laugh, run away from me and quickly become a little boy again. Every now and again he would also let himself get caught so he could get the hug I promised him.

When reactivity overpowers reflective thinking

When we are emotionally overwhelmed our reptilian brain kicks in. As mentioned in the previous chapter, our right brain, the emotional self, develops first, and continues as the entry point for all incoming sensory information (Schore 2001b; Van der Kolk 2014). Under threat, our lower order (survival) brain, acting as the gatekeeper, protects by summoning our defences which do not permit reflective thinking (Rifkin-Graboi *et al.* 2009). As a worker, when confronted with such powerful emotional states, we are susceptible to mirroring them, moving to lower order reactivity over higher order reflection. Our challenge is to make conscious our emotional states and then reflect on what possible meaning they may carry for us, and for others. This elevates our capacity to process, integrate and make sense of incoming information as we move up into our higher order (thinking) brain.

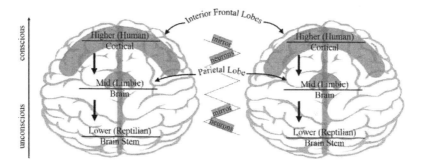

*Diagram 1 Hierarchy of Brain Functioning and
Triggering Emotional Reactions in Others*

However, moving to a reflective space during distressing or overwhelming emotional encounters is easier said than done. The following is a case example raised in a supervision session I facilitated and involves an infant aged only one month old and her first-time mother and other family members.

Case example: Constance (4 weeks) and Felicity (20)

A worker met with Felicity, a young mother, and her one-month-old daughter Constance. Felicity's parents and her older sister also attended the centre visit. The three additional family members in the room were highly anxious, as the mother was experiencing significant distress and had threatened to harm the infant and herself. The worker immediately became highly anxious about the welfare of the infant and observed that Constance was visibly distressed and difficult to soothe. The worker, a very competent and experienced practitioner, later described how overwhelmed she felt and explained how she had rushed about in the check-up session ensuring that the family had an extensive list of services to contact once they left her office. She also made a referral to both a local mental health service and a mother-infant residential unit. The worker was confident that the family members would ensure the physical safety of the infant and mother. She followed up referring the mother/infant dyad into the appropriate services. What remained for the worker were the feelings of helplessness and anxiety she felt for the infant, who was so clearly highly distressed, and her mother. The worker felt that she had let the infant down, perhaps mirroring the feelings of the mother and her fear of failing her infant.

The scenario captures good practice. The worker attended to the immediate practical concerns to ensure the safety and welfare of the mother and the baby. The worker did not minimise or dismiss their fears and acted promptly. What was missed, however, was the urgent need to attend to this infant's emotional safety. This scenario may have been considerably enhanced by looking to the youngest member of the group and reflecting on what the infant was letting the worker know, then and there, in the here and now. Making overt what the worker saw happening for the infant and striving to make sense of this may have been the most effective way of naming what all seemed to be feeling but struggled to make sense of. These were overwhelming and little-understood feelings which inhibited the adults' capacity to reflect on their own emotional state and make themselves available to help this small infant manage her distress.

Rather than one emotionally overwhelmed brain, the infant was surrounded by five dysregulated adults, flooded with anxiety, leaving no one able to think about her and her distress or to offer her what she needed in that moment. It was little wonder that the infant was so distressed. The psychological safety of the infant needed attending to as much as her physical safety. The worker joined the other adults in reacting rather than reflecting. While the worker's reactions were appropriate and ultimately helpful, the infant urgently needed someone to be able to think about and then help her caregivers manage this very young infant's overwhelming anxiety. Managing the infant's overwhelming anxiety is important because, in such circumstances, the infant's rapidly developing brain is being bombarded with potent chemicals which are intended to protect them when frightened. Should this bombardment continue unabated over lengthy periods of time, the infant brain's neural pathways are at risk of being negatively impacted in ways that may have far reaching developmental consequences. The danger facing the infant is that this 'frightening' relational experience inhibits other more helpful ways of living through complex emotions. This can lead to future difficulties in the development of higher order brain functioning as well as triggering anxiety in, rather enjoyment from, subsequent intimate relationships (Hesse & Main 2006; Schore 2003a). Furthermore, the infant who is 'frightened' within their primary caregiving relationship is left with nowhere to go as 'the parental behaviour inevitably places the infant in a behaviourally irresolvable situation in which the attachment figure simultaneously becomes both the haven of safety and the source of the alarm' (Hesse & Main 2006, p.310). Ultimately, what is most powerful to strive for is an understanding of what is frightening for both the infant and the caregiver.

Bringing down reactivity to heighten reflective thinking

It is possible to bring down heightened and distressing emotional states by recognising them. Put another way, this is by 'keeping mind in mind' (Allen *et al.* 2008, p.312). For the worker, foster carer or other adult in a caregiving role, this involves a commitment to understanding and calls for discipline and practice. Accessing regular reflective individual or group supervision (which some may call debriefing or consulting) is essential in this very challenging area of work. This is because reflective supervision helps us to think about our mind and the mind of others (see Chapter Eight).

Similarly, keeping informed through reading and training, and practising our ability to wonder about what we are feeling at any given time helps us learn to take an outside perspective on what we are feeling inside.

Had the worker reflected on her own feeling states, her right 'emotional' brain response would be able to move to integrate information across both brain spheres, leading to an elevation in higher order functioning, and restoring a capacity for reflection. Reflection offers opportunities to put into words what otherwise remains unconscious and out of awareness. We have a better chance of holding on to our capacity to think when we first acknowledge to ourselves that we feel anxious, and then question ourselves as to what's the anxiety about or where does it come from. We may then offer some meaningful communication which gives expression to what message or purpose the anxiety is providing.

Of course, at that exact moment, everyone in that room feared for the safety of the infant. Being able to not just fear the worst but to give ourselves permission to feel it, understand it, and then reflect on it creates a shift, and the chance to move through the anxiety and consider the options: that this can be thought about, talked about and given voice to. Being able to think opens up the possibility of being emotionally available to meet and validate the infant's distress so that she, the infant, is not left alone emotionally to manage something she is incapable of managing. By coming alongside the infant, and recognising and giving expression to how alone and afraid she must be feeling, Constance and the adults in the room may feel comforted and reassured, rather than swimming amidst the swirl of anxiety. This is something comparable to the old saying 'a problem shared is a problem halved'. However, for the infant it is so much more than this. Constance is learning, through every relational experience and encounter, how feelings feel, and how feelings are managed, or not managed. The worker had the chance to bring something new to this very potent and, for Constance, highly charged and implicit memory imprinting relational encounter. This makes possible an opening to deflate, even a little, this huge bubble of anxiety. This may have subsequently also lessened the anxiety of the other adults in the room.

The infant or child as the entry point

Speaking directly to the infant, gently, with a soothing voice, acknowledges the infant. I might say something like 'it must be very scary at the moment to have Mummy so upset and not feeling well', or 'I wonder what it feels like for you at the moment? I wonder how we can make you feel you will be ok and you are not alone'. This acknowledgment has the power to be immediately effective and potentially healing. The words may not be understood by the infant, but the adults will understand them, and the infant will understand the intonation and intention behind the words washing over them. The words offer the infant something to hold onto, through having their experience directly mirrored back and made sense of. The worker may reflect that 'I can feel how anxious everyone in the room feels right now. What can we as adults do to make this little one feel like she is safe, and that we are here for her and would like to soothe and comfort her'. When the worker puts the overwhelming emotions into language, the domain of the left brain, other adults in the room may be assisted to reclaim their own reflective capacities, and to then make themselves available to emotionally hold the infant. Further still, by engaging with the infant, as the person in the room most open to emotionally connecting, and assisting Constance to settle, we may offer an alternative and non-threatening mirror for these very concerned family members to look into.

This large group of adults with this very small baby had come to the worker so she could care for them all because they had lost their way. The number of family members accompanying the infant and mother attests to how anxious they all felt and just how tough this session would have been for any worker. I am not in any way under-estimating how distressing this session would have been for this professional. Nor am I proffering magical solutions. This is incredibly taxing work, for us all. However, by joining with and being caught up in the emotions of this anxious group, we run the risk of simply sending them off to the next service 'to take over'. As we know, the helping service system often gets caught up in the sense of impotence and fear of the families they serve, and it is not unusual for families to be sent on by the next service, to another and then another.

What the broader system reflects

The family violence sector can be plagued by a sense of powerlessness and not knowing what to do in the face of the 'unthinking' and violent actions of others. The opportunity to introduce news of difference and to create a shift does not require loads of additional money, resources or connections. Adequate funding and provision for ongoing and stable services should be, of course, mandatory (though it is often not). Fundamentally, however, we require a commitment to thinking about and to strengthening our capacity to reflect and to strive to make sense of those things that feel overwhelming, frightening and threatening. Holding on to rigid thinking, blaming others or looking to others to change rather than ourselves, an unwillingness to share limited resources, and setting services up against one another, all demonstrates how the system often mirrors the very client group we have been charged to work with.

Checking our own reflection

Now this is where it really gets hard. Looking at ourselves. Adults are better at telling children what to do and workers are similarly quick to impart advice and give direction to clients, though not always so fast to take it. A focus on what others must do differently over what we need to do differently is pronounced when working in an area such as family violence. This is because we can take, and are indeed sanctioned by society to take, the high moral ground. Ask anyone who has worked in large organisations or bureaucracies about the metaphorical blood-letting, bullying and cruelty that exists but is tidied up behind the doors of the human resources division. We are all part of the power struggles that exist within any relationship. What differs is the degree and extent to which we impose power over others.

Starting with ourselves

It is useful to start from the premise that the gap between ourselves and those we work with is not so wide. We appreciate being seen for who we believe we are and so too do our clients, even those who overtly use cruelty and violence in their relationships. Where the line needs to be drawn is around what are the baseline needs for an infant or young child to be physically and emotionally safe and to be physically and emotionally healthy. Starting with the infant and child and working upwards is a revolutionary idea for many. Generally, we think that by healing the parent we heal the child. This does not take into account the critical and immediate need for infants and young children, who cannot afford to wait, to be appropriately supported through significant periods of development. Parents can be calloused by years of trauma and there are no quick fixes, despite their often very real love and the best of intentions for their child. Infants and young children who have experienced and are still at risk of exposure to family violence require, as a baseline, the same things that every child deserves and needs to thrive:

- consistency of care

- additional supports in place (including access to the continuity of healthy relationships)

- physical and emotional safety, clean and stimulating environment

- to be spoken to, held securely, enjoyed, fed healthy foods and kept warm and clean

- access to appropriately supported developmental opportunities (kindergarten, primary school)

- opportunities for safe play and exploration.

Depending on for whom, and in what circumstances, this list was made, one could no doubt go further. My experience is that infants and young children are and often remain in sub-optimal circumstances even when child protection services are already involved with, or are well aware of, certain families. With regards to child protection, this may be because their hands are tied by the courts and statutory regulations. At times this is because of impossible workloads, inexperienced workers or a system which is overwhelmed and reactive. It does, however, become easy to blame child protection for not doing their job (why won't they remove the child?), or to blame them when they do (why did they remove the child?). In my practice, I have found it helpful to bring the question back to:

- What can I do now to make this infant or child's experience safe and positive?

- How do I create a space for his voice to be heard and to be respected?

- What are the baseline needs for this infant and/or child and how will they be met?

Asking these questions of yourself will be a clear step to keeping the infant and young child right here, right now, in your mind.

SETTING UP 'BASELINE NEEDS'

So, let's go back to the beginning. As a worker, foster carer, service or system, what is our baseline for working from the 'infant up'? What are the basics we need to ensure are met when working with families where there is violence, and what are the consequences when these are violated? That is, what boundaries do you place around the work you are doing with families where sometimes there are so few boundaries? Further, what have I put in place to ensure that how I practise makes explicit my commitment to infant- and child-led practice?

Case example: The Cherry Tree

An innovative program was established to work with high risk infants and their young mothers where concerns had been flagged by child protection either during pregnancy or immediately post-birth. The program was able to continue working with these young mothers throughout their child's early years. In addition to providing education, employment and life skills training to the mothers, The Cherry Tree program also provided intensive case management and advocacy support. The program soon found that the majority of the mothers had experienced violence both in their family of origin and their relationships as adults. This was either by the father of their child or a new partner. While many of the mothers demonstrated strong attachments to their children and their children to them, the workers noticed a pattern where several mothers continued to remain in intermittent contact with violent partners, or hid their ongoing relationships with violent partners from the team. Other challenges were continued bouts of substance use and 'going to ground', where for periods of time they would miss important appointments, not answer their mobiles and/or not be at home for scheduled visits. The program workers became increasingly disheartened. While finding some progress with these clients they also found lengthy patches where all their hard work seemed to go backwards and required their increased energy and commitment to re-engage these young mothers. When this happened everything would 'go to ground', with workers feeling like they were simply marking time until their clients would resurface and the work could begin again. This was made even harder by often disparate opinions held by other services, including child protection, about the mother's welfare.

The Cherry Tree staff were dedicated, hardworking and very skilful at engaging a cohort of young mothers who may not have otherwise engaged with services. They could maintain constructive and beneficial relationships with the mothers overall but, at times, the children got lost in the mix. Lengthy periods of time might go by where infants and small children were not sighted by staff, and where some young mothers went on benders and the welfare of the children was potentially compromised. Attendance at important appointments or stable child care placements was not always consistent, which raised worries about the child's safety. A number of these young mothers, themselves still immature and compromised by their own early childhood trauma were egocentric and, though they loved their children, they did not always make choices which put the interests of their children first. Many of them did not know how to do this. At times the workers from The Cherry Tree paralleled the mothers, by also not putting the needs of the children first. On occasion the workers gave too much leeway to these mothers for fear of losing what working relationship they did have, while some of the mothers rather expertly gave just enough to keep the workers and child protection satisfied, for fear of losing their children. The workers knew these mothers loved their children but they had little idea of creating safety around themselves or their children as they had had such little experience of this safety themselves. The workers felt disempowered when their wayward mothers went to ground and themselves felt like they had lost their way.

Imagine then what the children might be feeling. Just as the workers wanted these mothers to 'step up', so too did they need to. In working so hard to keep these very damaged mothers engaged, the workers, like their clients (the mothers) who returned to, or secretly maintained violent relationships, became fearful of losing the precarious relationships they had built. The mothers returned to traumatic relationships because that felt familiar and the workers, perhaps fearing they could not hold to these 'hard to keep' mothers, held on to what they could of the tenuous relationships they had built. What was not always happening was the workers putting the children first and foremost in their minds; the children continued to 'get lost' in the midst of all the other concerns.

The reason this program existed was to keep children in their mother's care. Clearly putting the infants and children front and centre, and ensuring that established *baseline needs* of the infants and children were met (as described above), sets up a different starting point to considering what are these mothers' baseline needs. Very clear expectations can be created, based not on privileging what the mother needs or wants, but what the infant needs in order to 'safely enough' remain in their mother's care. The rationale for doing so is to acknowledge that there is a baseline of care that infants do need and is imperative for healthy growth and development. When these *baseline needs* are not met, other adults need to step in to ensure the infant is not at risk of harm. Setting up clear expectations at the start need not preclude flexibility in how these needs are met, but prioritises the needs of the infant nevertheless. To not prioritise the infant's needs risks the accumulation of harm. All else flows from keeping the infant at the front of mind. This requires the worker to do their very best to help the mother keep the infant's basic needs in mind. There needs to be room to acknowledge error, as no caregiver gets it right all the time. As mentioned in Chapter Two (regarding 'match, mismatch and repair'), the real growth occurs in the process of working together to resolve that which is difficult (Tronick 2007). For many of these mothers this was not their experience growing up. The mothers often recalled their parent/s appearing to flip flop between either over-reacting by punishing or under-reacting by abandoning.

Establishing baselines

How this might look is informed by using an approach which sets out what are clear and non-negotiable needs necessary for every infant or child to survive and thrive, then working upwards. It is also important to expect and be prepared for lapses in the quality of care, but we need to have a clear commitment to think very carefully about anything that we suspect may not be good enough. The concept of the 'good enough' carer originated with Winnicott (1960) who suggested that when the quality of the care is 'not good enough', there is a major disruption to the infant's growing sense of self as they are too busy dealing with the 'consequences of that failure' (p.593). That is, the infant is required to cope with such disruptions in their care by defending themselves and adjusting their expectations and behaviours. Depending on the extent and/or damage caused by such disruptions to the infant's caregiving experience, growth will be stalled, as survival will always trump flourishing (Stern 2003).

It is both naïve and unrealistic to think this approach will be fool-proof, as nothing is, and particularly not in the fraught and complex of area of working to address family violence. This is about guidelines, while recognising, as with The Cherry Tree example above, that clients will make poor decisions, and re-enact behaviour that has served, albeit sometimes ineffectively, that which they have known for much of their lives. What might be different is how we respond to mother and infant and how we might help them find a way together that serves both well. This returns to the worker developing a way that makes explicit my commitment to infant- and child-led practice.

For example, should a mother want to remain in contact with a partner who is violent, it may be more effective to acknowledge this and endeavour to 'take the puff' out of such destructive and reactive relationships. This is not condoning remaining in a violent relationship. This is acknowledging that it may well happen irrespective of what we as workers want or say. But what is the baseline? The infant needs to remain safe and protected from harm. Child protection may or may have not have orders in place and women may or may not have intervention orders in place. Workers are often mandated to report child abuse, but if working with children and not mandated, this, I believe, remains as a non-negotiable pre-requisite for working with children and families. *We all have a responsibility to keep all infants and children safe. In my experience, this is our foundational commitment and obligation in any work where infants and children are involved.* However, how we define safety will often need discussion and reflection, because it is not always clear, particularly when a mother remains engaged in a violent relationship or repeats destructive behaviours towards herself or others.

The establishment of and commitment to the infant and/or child's *baseline needs* is perhaps the most important set of criteria to establish from the very beginning of any working relationship with parents. This takes considerable time in clarifying with parents just what we as workers will be watchful for. This baseline acts as a guide for you as a worker and for the parent. It also makes the expectations of the 'baseline needs' of the infant/child explicit. These needs may never have been so openly discussed, recognised or considered by the parent and can also be a powerful tool in revisiting and reflecting on some of their own early childhood traumas (see Chapter Seven).

Baseline	Plan	Negotiable
What ensures the infant or child's physical and emotional safety	What range of steps can be taken to ensure these are met	What are the areas which are negotiable and how can we support the parent's need for these without compromising the baseline

Diagram 2 Establishing Baselines

Not recognising the separateness of the infant or child from their mother or father can encourage unhelpful ways of working and may lead to an erroneous and unhelpful belief that all the child really needs is to be in the company of their mother (or father). This 'parent centric' way of thinking may add more pressure on to the caregiving adults who often already feel fragile and ill prepared for parenthood. Establishing baselines creates a space to reflect on what their infant or child needs to remain safe, cared for and healthy. This may be different to what they, as with the mothers in the case above, need or identify that they need (which may also be confused with what they want) in their lives. They may feel they need a big night out, but this is not something that would guarantee their infant remains safe or protected from frightening people or places.

An infant feels safe when they are not overwhelmed with people, places, sights and sounds that are intrusive or they may find startling. They need a caregiver who is responsive to their needs and protective of their physical and emotional safety. Talking in real terms about these possible clashes of interest, exploring options, like a reliable and safe alternative care placement for their child, may help the young mother think with you. Based on past experiences these young mothers may sometimes, or even often, feel compelled to 'act out' rather than 'think about' their emotional states. Talking with them about their choices can help deflate the urgency they may feel to re-enact what has 'worked', or at least allowed them to get away from their uncomfortable feelings, in the past.

Case example: Mia (30 months) and Sarah (19)

Mia's mother Sarah was just 16 when Mia was born. Sarah had come to the attention of child protection as she had been homeless throughout her pregnancy and police had escorted her to hospital as she was going into labour. Sarah identified that she had nowhere to live and no one to support her and the baby post the baby's birth. Sarah had been offered transitional, and then permanent, housing and had been provided with intensive support by The Cherry Tree staff since the birth of Mia. Sarah had initially been very difficult to engage and often missed appointments, but had gradually become more responsive and open to accepting help. Mia was now 30 months old and Sarah was 19. Sarah had been supported to return to a community-based school in the last twelve months where she was attempting to complete her final years of school. Sarah had a housing support worker and a very involved maternal child health nurse who had assisted Sarah to find a stable 'home-based child care' placement for Mia while she attended school. The Cherry Tree worker reported that Mia and Sarah enjoyed a loving relationship. However, it was since the home-based care placement had begun 12 months before that Mia had really started to thrive. Mia was rapidly developing her language and motor skills and exhibiting genuine excitement when dropped off each day at her placement. Sarah had the support from a community volunteer driver who provided daily help by dropping Mia off at her placement and picking her up at the end of each day.

Increasingly over the last six months, however, Sarah had begun missing days at school. A case conference was arranged with all the workers involved with Sarah and Mia. Sarah was invited to the meeting but elected not to attend. In the meeting, the information that Sarah had begun a relationship with Tom, one of her fellow students, was shared. Tom had a very troubled past and, while he had made great strides at the school, achieving high academic results, according to his school support worker he would occasionally 'go off the rails'. The school had heard rumours from other students that Tom had on one occasion threatened to 'kill Sarah' if he ever found her with another man. Sarah had recently informed her housing worker that she wished to move to the country with Mia and start a new life with Tom. She was contemplating dropping out of the community school to pursue plans to become a hairdresser.

While there were plenty of concerning developments in Sarah's life, there were no clear or immediate protective concerns for Mia. The workers felt uncertain as to what action to take and, while they were keen to discourage the relationship between Sarah and Tom, they felt helpless as to know how. Looking through the lens of what Sarah wanted and felt she needed, the community school worker and the housing support worker believed they needed to support Sarah in her aspirations, even if they did not fully agree with them. Their fear was that if they confronted her by expressing their concerns they risked losing her.

The maternal child health nurse and The Cherry Tree worker believed that Sarah was a good parent and that Mia and Sarah had a strong and positive attachment. The volunteer driver was committed to supporting Mia's attendance at her day care placement, as she could see how much pleasure and benefit Mia derived from her time spent there. The struggle for the workers was how to support Sarah when her plans would jeopardise Mia having her safe base.

From an infant-led perspective, Mia needed the continuity of the relationships offered to her by the day care placement as well as the volunteer driver. The facilitation of the 'home-based child care' placement had obviously provided Mia, and her mother, with important developmental and emotional supports and was available to them both for another 18 months. In shifting from an adult centric, Sarah-focused approach to focus on what Mia's development and behaviour was telling us she needed, led to realigning the baseline. It is completely understandable that Sarah wanted a relationship, a new career, a new life. However, she was Mia's mother and was responsible for Mia and her developmental needs. Developmentally, it seemed critical that Mia remain in her placement and Sarah seemed to have lost sight of the ways her role as a parent was directly supported through Mia's attendance at this day care placement. Mia remaining in her placement was assessed by this group as a baseline need. All other requirements were considered negotiable.

The plan to keep Mia at day care formed the basis for working on a plan with Sarah to achieve her aspirations. These included such things as how she might explore other feasible living arrangements with her housing worker which still enabled her, or the volunteer driver, to get Mia to day care for at least for the next 12, preferably 18, months. Hairdressing and other different courses could be explored through her school support worker. If Tom was to share a home with Sarah and Mia, it was then important for The Cherry Tree worker to help Tom in his transition into either a parental role or adult role, in sharing a home with Mia and her mum.

Given her age, stage and vulnerability, it was imperative for Mia to be placed at the centre of planning and future considerations. This needed to become the explicit pre-requisite for the group of support workers to continue working with Sarah and with Mia. Discussion and negotiation with Sarah was vital, but the group of workers needed to advocate for what was best for Mia and to support Sarah in accepting this. Mia's developmental need to continue with her current day care arrangement was the only non-negotiable arrangement; all others could be worked towards together. Should this point not be one that Sarah could agree to then the workers were clear where their responsibilities would lie. The baseline might change from the worker's perspective (for example, how Tom may feature in the future of Mia and Sarah's life), but what could not change was clarity around Mia's need for stability and emotional and physical safety in her relationships with others.

MAKING NOTIFICATIONS

Most workers are filled with dread at the prospect of making a notification to child protection. We feel like we become the bad guy (a fear I have heard workers express repeatedly) and that the parent/s will detest us. This appraisal of our actions – being the 'bad guy' – replicates the anxiety parents feel about how they are judged as parents, and suggests a rigidity of thinking that labels certain behaviours as good, and as bad. Notifying does not always sever relationships with the clients we work with and I have found that it sometimes strengthens them. It is perhaps our resistance to notifying that indicates how adult centric we may be. This is when we feel a greater concern about what it means for the parent to risk losing their child, than what it may mean for the infant or child should they stay.

The decision to report to child protection, or police, can also often feel precarious as well as unclear, as not all workers see 'unacceptable risk' in the same way. This is always the reality when working with families where there is violence. Ultimately, the determination of unacceptable risk is child protection's call, and we will either be told or given evidence of their assessment in due course. You may need to learn how to find a clear voice and to develop your capacity to become a strong advocate for children, and to become fearless in applying pressure on other services to also report.

At times we may exhaust all possibilities and still find infants and children are left in unacceptable situations. We need to make this explicit and document, document, document, and communicate our concerns, in writing, to others. Sometimes we need to take action by contacting those in statutory positions of higher authority. Being honest and explicit from the outset can help assist our work, whatever our role – therapist, support worker, case manager, foster carer or kinship carer. Our confidentially with any client is not bound by any matters we consider might place infants and children in harm's way. I have yet to have a client decline to work with me after I make clear from the outset that within the state where I live within Australia I am mandated to report when infants and children are at risk. I also tell them that even if I was not required to by legislation I would still report, because as an adult it is my responsibility to help keep infants and children safe. I believe being honest from the start provides a secure base for the client to work from.

We know that for some children who remain in less than ideal circumstances, regular attendance at a good child care centre, respite placement, staying with extended family, and pre-school or school for older children, can be enormously beneficial. These other settings and relationships may provide a level of constancy in the lives of some children which they would otherwise not have, offering an environment where the child thrives and finds his or her needs more consistently met. There may be kith and kin who offer important relationships that need to be protected and nurtured. Children need help to safely remain in contact with fathers and mothers who have used violence where the infant or child expresses a desire to stay connected, or through their behaviours demonstrate that there are positive benefits from remaining connected in some way. This includes our ability to allow children to talk about what they think, feel and want in relation to certain relationships, despite our misgivings. There will be instances where contact is neither practical, safe nor in the child's best interest. However, sometimes our job is to make sure that connection is as safe and as constructive as it possibly can be. Conversely, infants and children communicate volumes through their behaviour and emotional states when they feel afraid of, or simply do not want to have contact with, certain caregivers. All too often infants and/or children's behavioural and emotional protests are ignored as workers (and legal representatives) clamour to ensure 'the rights of the parent'.

Reading these last two paragraphs may have left you feeling exhausted. Making some of these relational opportunities available to infants and children may feel like climbing a very slippery, hazardous and dangerous mountain. As with climbing a mountain, everything rests with safety as the base. In my experience, these ideals are seldom afforded the infant or young child. Our commitment to placing the infant at the centre of our concern and considering the infant and their communications and needs is the beginning of changing practices that in the past have all too often overlooked the infant. Infants' and young children's needs and rights have been overlooked, leaving them without a voice and without consideration. We need to be creative in how we keep some non-custodial parents connected and respected as the parents of their children.

Completely cutting out parents from children's lives does not always guarantee children's safety in the long run. I have worked with many children and adolescents who were removed from home, albeit too late in some instances, only to abscond and return home repeatedly once they were physically able to. We need to find better ways to think about and honour children's attachments, be they for better or for worse, and facilitate how these relationships can be managed safely. A foster carer recently told me how she had sent the mother of the foster care child she cares for a 'Mother's Day' card. This foster carer imagined this mother had had little recognition of her role as mother. This small but thoughtful and genuine gesture set in motion a series of shifts in their relationship where this foster mother and mother formed a workable caregiving relationship for the sake of the child. We do not hear enough of these good stories, perhaps because we often fail to reflect on the feeling states of the other and try to make sense of their experience and their place in a child's heart or mind.

FOUNDATIONS FOR PRACTICE

We sometimes find ourselves behaving towards particular people we work with or care for in ways which are uncharacteristic of how we would usually behave. We can find ourselves 'acting out' in the face of unlikeable, unappealing and constantly difficult clients. Adults and/or children who have experienced considerable trauma may find it difficult to make conscious the thoughts that are unthinkable. These might include painful insights like 'my mother wished that I had not been born', 'I do not love, or even like my child', 'I would rather have my partner stay than risking him or her leaving if I stop him/her hitting my child' or 'I was born because of my mother being raped'. We too can find ourselves having thoughts we think we should not have about the very children and families we are meant to assist. We all need to develop a capacity for facing these thoughts, being curious about them and finding ways to reflect on them, as well as living with uncomfortable, ambivalent and painful feelings. My hope is that this book will help you do just that.

Self-care

It is extremely difficult to witness many of the dynamics we see in our work. Looking into the face of the infant who simply stares with vacant eyes, or seeing the toddler who is told to 'suck it up' when they hurt themselves, or the young child who flails about trying to manage their younger sibling's behaviour as their parent/s sits nearby unperturbed, is very hard to watch. Imagine how it feels for the child left alone to manage the emotional states which accompany such situations. While reading this book you may be able to recall images (and feelings) that still haunt you from your experience of working with or caring for infants and children and their families. Memories, both painful and joyous, of the many infants and children I have worked with remain with me.

Working with infants and children is right and left brain work. The ideal is for the two hemispheres to work together (McGilchrist 2011). We need to be able to connect with our emotional selves, and reflect on what our emotions are telling us in order to sit with/bear and make sense of what our clients are telling us. There needs to be a bridge (like our corpus callosum – in Chapter Two) which aids the integration of the theory into our practice (i.e., right and left brain working together). The sturdiness and capacity of this bridge, I think, rests on the quality of the key connecting practice principles necessary for undertaking this challenging, complex and often (highly) anxiety provoking area of work. Rather than looking immediately at what we want to change in our client's lives, I would suggest that in every encounter we begin with reflecting on ourselves. How do we, as workers, or perhaps substitute carers, 'slow down' to 'work faster'? We can make a huge difference in what we offer the traumatised child by remaining reflective about, and not over-reacting to, our own emotional states and anxiety. As you begin to truly see them and feel their emotional states, whatever they may be, you offer the traumatised infant or child access to a very different, and potentially inviting and positive relational experience.

We are helped by approaching this work with certain beliefs and self-directed questions to guide what, why and how we do what we do. These go towards helping us to develop a great capacity for 'mentalising' (as discussed in Chapter Two). Jeremy Holmes, a British psychiatrist and psychotherapist, explains mentalisation as being able to remain mentally present, the willingness and ability to see others from the inside and yourself from the outside (Allen *et al.* 2008). This involves recognising how we come across to and impact upon our clients through how we feel and behave. When dealing with the complexities inherent in family violence work, our ability to remain reflective in the face of distressing emotions and events offers the infant/child and family the quickest route to safer ground.

DEVELOPING PRINCIPLES TO GUIDE INFANT- AND CHILD-LED PRACTICE

A quote I value, and which is attributed to American philosopher Jacob Needleman, notes that the trouble we get ourselves into is not because of the questions we ask but rather the answers we find. This quote refers to our focus on and obsession with answers. When we become too 'hard and fast' in our views we obscure possibilities for new and helpful ways of thinking. Infants and small children have so much to teach us. They are often much more interested in questions than answers. Curiosity and the mutuality of discovery, and coming to know the world of the infant or child together with the infant, child and their caregivers, is vital to infant- and child-led practice. Once we are convinced we know, we abandon our capacity for discovery. As such, the list of proposed practice principles provided below, as well as the 'self-directed' questions to follow, is neither absolute, nor finite. They are drawn from my knowledge of the research and theory and what I have learnt from my own practice and reflected upon in my own individual supervision over many years.

Guiding practice principles

- This work is vital, and neurodevelopmentally urgent for the infant.

- Infants and young children have their own subjective experiences.

- Infants and children deserve to live free of harm, abuse and exploitation.

- The infant is totally, and the young child highly, dependent on their caregiving environment.

- The caregiving environment is fundamental to whether the infant or child thrives, survives or dies.

- Keeping the infant or child safe is as much about their emotional wellbeing as it is their physical and environmental wellbeing.

- Infant- and child-led work occurs in the context of respecting and helping to strengthen their relationships with those who care for them.

- It is important to respect, observe and learn about the relational attachments of infants and children.

- It is important to be open to what the infant and young child can teach us.

- We need to actively invite infants and children to be part of all our working relationships.

- Being blind to or colluding with 'adult centric' practices comes at an unacceptable cost to the infant and young child.

- 'Coming to know' rather than being 'all knowing' opens our minds and relationships up to mutual discovery.

- Being present to discover and give meaning to the relationships we form with infants, young children and their carers is best supported by giving attention to our own journeys of discovery, through reflective individual/

peer/group supervision, ongoing professional development and a constant commitment to learning.

This last principle will be discussed in more detail in Chapter Eight.

The following questions are intended to support us in becoming clearer about the principles we practise by. As with the practice principles, these lists of questions are purposefully offered as guidelines. I have found them helpful in informing my day-to-day work as a practitioner, group supervisor and someone who trains others in infant- and child-led approaches.

Questions to support our practice

Some useful questions include:

- Can I keep my mind open and be emotionally available to what it feels like to be present with this infant?

- Can I act to facilitate the emotional and physical safety of this infant or child?

- Do I respect the attachments of this infant or child while ensuring their safety is not compromised?

- What can I do to foster greater emotional connection and mutual enjoyment within the mother (and/or father) and baby relationship?

- How might I enhance a mother's and/or father's capacity to respond to their baby's communication?

- How might I facilitate both the capacity for and opportunities to enjoy affectionate gaze?

- How might I facilitate shared connections and intimacy between this infant or child and the adults important in their caregiving world?

- Can I be honest and ask the hard questions as well as hear and reflectively act, not react, when I hear answers, even when I don't like them?

- Can I use myself and my relationship with both infant/child and carer to encourage their capacity to experience each other in a new and more positive way?

- Can I use my relationship with both infant or child and carer to help them recognise and begin to tolerate emotions which may feel frightening and overwhelming?

- What can I do to enhance my capacity to remain reflective in the presence of overwhelming emotions that can confront me when undertaking infant- and child-led practice where there is family violence?

- Can I make space to wonder about the voice of the child? What stops me?

- How can I introduce and share play with this mother and infant?

Applying an infant- and child-led approach to families struggling to manage, even in the absence of known violence, is hard enough. It gets even harder when an infant or child is at immediate risk of harm, but it is still very important to consider the infant when it seems there is only time for swift action. Some workers and involved others will lament that action to safeguard the children was not swift enough in some cases. There are seldom easy or straightforward answers and the emotional burden of this work is considerable. Yet, every step along the way can be thought about by asking ourselves 'what potential meaning will this infant or child make of this experience and what impact might this have on their emotions and their relationships?', and 'in what way can these necessary actions be done to best support the emotional experience and states of the infant or child?' Another way to consider this is to ponder the question, 'if this infant or this child could tell me in plain language how they felt and what they wanted, now and in their future, what do I imagine this would be?'

SUMMARY

Gaining confidence in connecting directly with infants and children, and seeing them as equal participants in your work in addressing family violence, can radically change the way we practise. Ensuring that their baseline needs are met can mirror what are all too often the baseline needs of their parents. That is, the need for safe relationships, continuity and the ability to manage distressing emotions and thoughts with reflection not reactivity. The shift to being infant- and child-led workers requires a shift in the way we think and the way we practise. It begins not with the other, but within ourselves.

Chapter Four

Interventions that attend to the infant or child's experience of trauma, their emerging sense of self, the meaning they make of themselves and of others and their primary attachments, are crucial if our work is to offer reparative experiences. These reparative experiences are necessary to address the impact of early, violent disruptions in family relationships that impinge on and impair healthy developmental trajectories.

Our work is situated not in creating activities 'to do' with infants and children, but in learning how 'to be' with them. A therapeutic relationship with someone who was neither part of nor affected by these traumatic experiences can help facilitate their growth in developing healthy ways of how to be with themselves, and with others.

Making Meaning in the Context of Family Violence

Within the context of ongoing family violence, how the infant makes meaning is different to how the older, verbal child makes meaning. As the child develops, so too does their capacity to defend themselves, in constructive or less than constructive ways. The feelings of anguish, fear or distress associated with frightening events do not change. What changes is how these events are processed and managed. Keeping the infant and child front and centre, involving them directly in all work and seeking to hear their voice and to help others to hear and attend to the infant or child's communication, sits at the heart of any work when taking an infant- or child-led approach. This chapter is about looking to infants and children to teach us how to best support them, their relationships and their meaning-making. Specific to work with family violence is managing the anxiety and fear that accompanies working with a family system where the threat of violence continues to loom large or, at the very least, to powerfully linger. Most significantly, what sets this work apart from other work is the insidiousness with which family violence permeates the very relationships intended to protect and teach the infant and child about themselves and others and the way the world works. It compromises the sense they make of and for themselves, and of others.

As is often the case, when the violence commences in utero and/or in early infancy, memories are imprinted by their physiological experiences, and these memories remain, implicit and pre-verbal. This means that they are not conscious memories that can be thought about and talked about, but that they lie hidden in the developing brain, influencing the physiological memories that remain active in the body.

Psychiatrist Bessel Van der Kolk (2014) suggests that trauma, at whatever age it is experienced, is stored non-verbally, making it extremely difficult for the individual to put their experiences into words. As mentioned in Chapter Two, Broca's area, a speech centre in the brain, is affected when we are overwhelmed by fear. Interestingly, therapeutic work with very young children, including those whose language has not developed, clearly demonstrates that play can offer a window into early relationship experiences, offering the therapist important information and details about traumatic events in the children's early lives (Emanuel 2011; Jordan 2011). These experiences may also be illuminated through what Freud called 'repetition compulsion' and which since has been written about extensively by others (Box *et al.* 1981; Chu 1991; Van der Kolk 1989). Repetition compulsion refers to an unconscious process where 'many traumatised people expose themselves, seemingly compulsively, to situations reminiscent of the original trauma. These behavioural re-enactments are rarely consciously understood to be related to earlier life experience' (Van der Kolk 1989, p.389). This suggests a need for us to discover what the infant or child is telling us non-verbally, and what their parents may also be showing us about their earliest experiences in the world through the way they behave and the way they parent.

This chapter will look at how to work with infants, toddlers, young children and their families in our attempts to bring about healing. How to safely make traumatic experiences conscious will be explored, along with ways to usefully make sense of this harm. How to access that which has been relegated to the bunker (see Chapter Two) and which continues to act as the emotional, relational and behavioural command centre during times of crisis will be explained. This work involves not simply engaging with the child's hurt, but demands we find a way to enter the bunker and help extend the possibilities for their safe self-expression. We do this through finding words for and making meaning of feelings, memories and behaviours which have not made sense, and which can build pathways towards self-awareness.

STARTING AT THE VERY BEGINNING

The client group we are concerned with are those who have been exposed to and/or have been the direct recipient of violent relational behaviours. Most often by someone with whom they have an intimate or primary relationship. For many, these relational violations began at the very beginning of their lives. Such a start in life leads to instabilities carried forth in all subsequent relational encounters, and the expectation that you too may cause them harm. This fear will influence how they relate to you and to others. It is incredibly helpful to try and reflect on what might lie behind any problematic behaviours from the outset. This involves understanding that for children, as well as adults, 'these problematic "acting-out" or "acting-in" behaviours stem from neither a desire for attention nor a compulsion to misbehave, but instead from the instinctive need to self-protect' (Bunston 2017, p.405). This does not condone those behaviours which involve violence, but seeks to understand their origin and their function.

Learning to observe

In the world of counselling and casework the worker is taught to really listen. This involves sometimes hearing the story behind the words. What is equally important is learning to really see by observing. This involves seeing what may lie beneath what you are watching. Observation is about entering the non-verbal world and engaging all our senses to absorb what is happening around us. The world of the infant is best understood through observation, and through how we 'engage with them, allowing ourselves to feel the sympathetic response that the other's actions and feelings invite' (Reddy & Trevarthen 2004, p.9). A method of training in the psychoanalytic infant mental health field is known as 'infant observation'. This method was developed nearly seventy years ago through the work of Ester Bick, a child psychoanalyst (Bick 1964, 1986). Bick was asked by John Bowlby (who pioneered attachment theory) to set up a program for trainees to understand the development of infants and their experience (Rustin 2009). Infant observation training involves watching the minute behaviours of the infant, capturing every moment and every emotion. These 'observation' sessions occur in the natural environment of the infant, generally their home. Then, immediately post session, students are required to write rigorous notes on what they saw and what they felt.

Within mother–infant, father–infant or caregiver–infant interactions, the focus is not so much on what is said as on the way in which they relate to one another. The imperative on the observer is not to judge but to watch, and 'repeatedly allows him/herself to be affected by the experience' (Caron *et al.* 2012, p.229). The observation component of this formalised training method is generally one hour a week which occurs over a substantial period (12 months or longer). Additionally, this is generally with the same infant and their caregivers, and with the observer remaining respectfully present but non-intrusive. The process notes written after each visit serve as the basis for reflection and discussion in a formal weekly supervision group of three to five participants and a final written paper may also be required.

Initially established for the training of psychoanalytically informed child psychotherapists, infant observation is now used in training many disciplines. It is also used as a research tool, and within different settings and with many different ages and population groups (Adamo 2008; Fleming 2004; Hughes & Heycox 2005; McKenzie-Smith 2009; Rustin 2006). Not everyone who works with infants and children will have the opportunity to undertake such training but everyone has the opportunity to learn from the principles of infant observation practice. As mentioned in Chapter Two, the approach of 'Watch, Wait, Wonder' uses observation (Cohen 2006). This encourages both workers and adult parents/caregivers to not simply react to the infant but watch what the infant is doing, think about what they are seeing and wonder about the infant's experience. 'Watch, Wait, Wonder' is pressing the pause button in order to fully take on board all the information being offered by the infant: visually, gesturally, vocally, behaviourally and emotionally (Cohen 2006; Cohen *et al.* 1999; Cohen *et al.* 2002).

When feelings are felt

Within the context of family violence, allowing yourself permission to feel what you are seeing in the infant is painful, sometimes distressingly so, but also enormously illuminating, and ultimately helps facilitate healing. This act of genuinely connecting with the feeling states of the infant offers them an experience of another who cares for them, and this is very important for the infant's healthy development. It offers them a validating emotional exchange where they are not alone, and have an interested other, who is trying to understand what they feel inside. This creates an 'inter-subjective' relational experience (what happens between two people) where the infant and their parent, or an infant and you, together create shared meaning (Ammaniti & Gallese 2014; Beebe & Lachmann 1998; Stern 2003; Stolorow 1994). What the infant receives is a congruent response to what they feel on the inside about what is happening on the outside, and they can store this exchange in their growing library of physiological memories. These earliest memories contribute directly to their evolving core self. This back and forward exchange takes something meaningful from the other, and offers something meaningful back. It is essentially what is created between two, not what is created by one or by the other, which makes this exchange meaningful. The infant who does not experience something meaningfully returned in their relational exchanges experiences what is known as a 'mismatch', as was described in Chapter Two (Tronick 2001). This leaves the infant alone to try to make meaning of and manage something emotionally complex. As Tronick and Beeghly (2011) explain:

> Infants and young children have a stunning array of biopsychosocial competencies. Even young infants have rudimentary intentions and organized and motivating emotions and are able to react to the meanings of others' intentions and emotions...their meaning-making is nonsymbolic and radically different from the representational meaning made by older children and adults,

but it is meaning nonetheless. Unfortunately, in ways unique to infants, their meaning-making may go wrong and may lead down aberrant developmental pathways. (p.107)

When incongruent behaviour and/or an emotional expression is offered back to the infant, such as the angry parent smiling back, a parent offering no reaction or remaining expressionless to a distressed infant, a mismatch between what the infant feels and what the infant sees in their parent's expression occurs. The infant is at risk of the mismatch being internalised if this is often repeated and no repair is offered. Over time, this negatively impacts the infant's ability to not only read and manage other people's emotional expressions, but in managing their own.

Case example: Jed (24 months) and Chrissy (27)

Jed was running around the room, darting from one toy to another when he tripped over his shoelace and went sprawling across the floor. His mother Chrissy was sitting cross-legged on the floor searching through her handbag. She did not look up when Jed started to howl as she was intent on finding something in her purse. Jed picked himself up and limped over to her, still crying. He stopped short of reaching out for her and as she looked up, clearly agitated, she said to him, 'stop being a girl'. Jed quietened, turned to me and looked at my face and I gave him a pained expression and I let out a low 'ouch'. I also sat on the floor and was still for a moment watching the both, feeling sad at what seemed like a missed opportunity for closeness. Chrissy eventually looked up, seemingly suddenly aware of the silence. I spoke to them both saying, 'I wonder what hurt Jed most. Falling over, or you calling him a girl?'

This small exchange was pivotal and was to offer a rich reservoir of material to work with during our time of working together. Jed was doing what every child does when distressed. He sought comfort. At the age of two an infant is incapable of managing their emotional states on their own and he had really hurt himself. Chrissy experienced Jed's distress as weak and demanding. She expected him to do just what she had learnt to do in her life, to look after himself. Together we could explore how she asked for help when she needed it and whether what she got back from others in her life was satisfying. We could explore what sort of man she wanted her son to grow into and how she would help him grow into this sort of man. Chrissy and I got better at capturing those exchanges between her and her son as they happened in the moment. We could then use them to reflect on with Jed, and to give them real, congruent and coherent meanings, so as to provide Jed with the building blocks with which to begin to make sense of himself and his world.

Case example: Samuel (3 months old), Clara (36 months old) and Shiala (34)

Shiala was the mother of five children. She had entered a refuge with her children after her youngest son, Samuel, just three months old, was caught in the crossfire of an ugly altercation with her partner where she was slammed into a wall while holding Samuel. After years of violence this event led to Shiala leaving her partner for the first time. Shiala had agreed to join a small group for infants and mothers being run in the refuge. Shiala's spoken English was very poor and an interpreter had been employed for the group. Shiala presented as somewhat lethargic and, while both Samuel and her older daughter Clara were included in the group, she paid Clara scant attention and focused what energy she did have into holding Samuel. They appeared to have a positive relationship, with Samuel often looking up at his mother and receiving warm smiles and the occasional fragments of a softly sung lullaby. The refuge workers and I wondered aloud about how frightening it must have been to consider that in that violent, split second moment, Shiala may have lost her beloved baby. We also wondered how frightened Samuel may have felt then and how safe he appeared to feel now.

Clara entertained herself with a new packet of pencils and some paper given to her by the refuge staff. She seemed very wary of the other children and adults in the group. During a warm-up song, she took herself away from the group to a little table nearby, and despite a number of overtures made to her by others to join in with the group she kept herself at a safe distance. When I reflected on why Clara might seem to prefer to keep herself at a safe distance, Shiala commented that, 'Clara likes to keep things for herself and is not good at sharing.' Not long after this an older brother of Clara's who had been playing with staff in an outside play area bounded into the room to ask his mother something. As he was leaving he spied Clara's pencils and, before she could stop him, he grabbed two of them and ran out of the room. Clara became teary and moved hesitantly towards her mother and looked ready to howl.

Shiala stretched out one arm, held up her palm and said, 'Shush.' Clara stopped in her tracks, her whole, tiny body shuddering. She seemed to heave a cry in silence then turned around and went back to her table. I looked on in horror. I have no recollection of what I said. I do recall feeling horrendous and helpless, and I still do when I recall that memory. I wanted to reach out to Clara and comfort her but felt I had neither her nor her mother's permission to do so. I was stuck to the spot and I remember looking at her plaintively wishing she would look my way so she could look into my eyes and know I saw and felt her pain. But she did not.

This case example offers an example of the very real visceral (gut level) angst felt in undertaking this work. Later, speaking to refuge staff who participated in the group, they reported that Shiala had not been feeling well, but despite this she got a great deal from being part of the group. They discovered more about Shiala in that one session than they had learnt about her in the two weeks she had been at the refuge. The staff members also felt the group experience had offered them a chance to see what infant- and child-led practice involved. I was left feeling disappointed that I had not recovered in time to do something more healing with the exchange I witnessed between Clara and her mother. I also acknowledged to myself that I was mirroring back something powerful in that room which remained primitive but I was unable to verbalise. I did not simply swipe this away but allowed myself to experience these punishing sensations fully, and, perhaps, Clara felt a little less alone in that room. That was my hope. I also felt hope that the positive shifts the staff reported back gave the staff an opportunity to further develop the work which began in that group with both Shiala and Clara. Ultimately, however, after witnessing that exchange I was left with an overwhelming emotional memory with no satisfactory resolution, as too, I suspect, was Clara.

TALKING ABOUT VIOLENCE IN FRONT OF INFANTS AND SMALL CHILDREN

While there may be occasions where speaking about the violence infants and children have experienced in front of them is not appropriate, this is generally not the case. These infants and children have seen the violence, felt it, smelt it, heard it and lived it. Rather than the content itself being problematic, it is the narrative of how what has occurred unfolds through the telling which can create further distress or can bring relief. In these circumstances, much rests with how the worker asks questions, as well as listens and responds to what they are being told. Early in my work with clients I was not ready to hear some things, so I was not told them. As I gained in experience, and in learning, I began to hear snippets of information which invited me to go beyond the surface. I began to watch faces more intently and think about what was *not* being said. This is again the 'inter-subjective' experience that is created through the relational exchange which occurs in the sharing/telling (verbally and non-verbally) and in the receiving/listening.

When infants and children are involved in and present during the telling of stories about what has happened to them and to their mother (or father), they have the opportunity to not only share their experience but to have that experience mediated, validated and thought about, instead of just reacted to. The complicated attachments infants and children share with both their mother and father, or same sex parents, and their complex feelings can be given expression while being supported by the worker. Incredibly conflicting and confusing behaviours and emotions can be unpacked constructively, such as those expressed by a young boy I worked with who said, 'I love to go fishing with my dad but when he was at home he sometimes used to hit Mum and that made me so angry with him.' Children (and even infants) can be supported in their positive and negative feelings towards one or both parents in a space where they are given permission to express their point of view.

Honouring children's attachments

Parents who are openly hostile about their child's other parent can, with thoughtful engagement and sensitive reflection, be supported to respect their child's attachment to that parent and to find ways to keep what is precious about that attachment/relationship protected. This is critically important to the infant and child's emerging sense of self. They are biologically and psychologically tied to this 'original couple' who produced them:

> Every infant will have their own experience, memories, feelings, and fantasises about their father and their mother and also her introjections regarding the violence witnessed and/or experienced themselves. If her father has left or abandoned them, or been removed from living in the home, there may be conflicted feelings of perhaps dissociation, numbness, or relief, mixed with guilt, sadness, and loss at being separated from her father. It is our role as therapists to help infants and mothers to try to separate what belongs to each of them and to recognise their experiences as being different. Clinicians need to be able to think about the intense feelings left in the abused mother/father, with the possibility that such feelings may also be projected onto the child. (Jones & Bunston 2012, p.228)

The alliances or attachments children form with different family members can leave the young child feeling split in two. If they want to continue contact with one parent, despite what has transpired between their parents, it can leave the other parent feeling betrayed and abandoned. This is particularly so for young boys who may want to have continued contact with their father but remain in the care of their mother. The bleed from this anger between the parents spreads across all the familial relationships and can be toxic. This toxicity is further amplified when there are siblings who align solely with the mother, or where they have different fathers. Helping families to tolerate, rather than criticise each other's alliances is tough work to say the least. Should the family have been able to find this tolerance for themselves, then they are unlikely to be seeking our support.

The very different meanings made of pivotal events in families are complex enough even where no violence is involved. Collective memories vary. Should they be similar, one family member processes the same event in a vastly different way to another family member. It may feel deeply shameful for a young boy to want to go fishing with his dad or to have any contact with him. Particularly when other family members refuse to see this boy's father because of his violence. Rather than be supported to talk through these complexities together, they go underground, and may be released destructively through 'acting out' behaviours. The little boy who wants to see his dad may tantrum or become aggressive. He cannot make sense of his conflicted feelings towards his father when his mother cannot tolerate hearing him in any way supporting his father or in any way behaving like his father. The more his mother tells him that he is 'just like his dad', the more shamed he becomes and his feeling states overwhelm him. As noted in the previous chapter in relation to the mirroring of emotions, this escalation in anxiety shuts down thinking and increases defensive behaviours. This is not simply modelling his father's behaviour. This is a young boy's inability to make sense of what he feels on the inside with what he sees and does on the outside.

By talking through complex and emotionally challenging material with the infant or child in the room, the worker can help mediate the distressing emotions that accompany the re-telling of upsetting events. Our listening can help to break down what are unpalatable conscious and unconscious memories. It can also free the child from having to carry the visceral traumatic memories that they are ill-equipped to make sense of. The worker, foster carer or supportive adult can try and put into words what seems impossible and intolerable to state. For example, it may be possible to gently recognise some of the troubled ties that bind each of these family members to each other. Every mother became involved with every father and at some point, perhaps, even felt she could fall in love, did fall in love, or may be ashamed to acknowledge she may still feel in love with him. Perhaps there was never love but together they produced a child and this child feels loving feelings towards both of them and sometimes may feel angry feelings towards both of them. Perhaps this parent can imagine their child both loving and hating them, at the same time, as maybe they have felt about their mother or father. Perhaps they have felt this about themselves. These 'hard to have' conversations are about loosening up the tight grip that shame and frightening feelings have on the internal and external functioning of families familiar with violence. More so, it encourages the possibility of open dialogue continuing beyond that which occurs with the worker. The importance of speaking about violence in front of the child is not about what is said so much as how it is being said and how we listen to what we are being told. This inter-subjective exchange offers a different experience because it is received differently by us. We can help with managing the feelings generated by and meanings attributed to these events, and perhaps with creating new ways to think.

Learning to listen

Imagine a curt police officer taking down a factual statement of what happened and where. Or a person going to court and being grilled about the facts of the case by an aggressive lawyer about what the victim of the violence did or did not do to provoke the attacker. Applying for financial assistance or housing support can all call for a re-telling of the story, sometimes to a hostile or disbelieving audience. Listening with all your senses, and imagining what it feels like to be that person offers a very different relational experience, and may make them feel like they are telling the story for the first time. This is because you are not simply listening, but you are thinking about what it is they are saying and not saying and about how they are feeling beneath the words.

Our interest in the infant's experience ushers in a new voice which will tell us when parents or other adults are behaving poorly, just as quickly as parents tell us about the poor behaviour of their children. Entering into the quagmire of family work in relation to family violence requires an ability to hold multiple perspectives, as you endeavour to untangle the emotional threads that so powerfully and frighteningly hold these families so tightly together. When we are working with mothers and their children alone we need to hold an understanding of the complex feelings children feel towards both parents, and not just their absent fathers and/or stepfathers.

VIOLENT ATTACHMENTS

Violence at the hands of someone you loved or may still love is not simply explained away as the misuse of power and the exertion of control. This is far too simplistic a description of the deeply etched relational tugs that pull within us. Using violence in intimate relationships can also be more deeply understood as an exaggerated or highly immature form of protest. The intention is to keep someone near at the very point when their departure is feared. The anxiety may be that the person is about to be abandoned or left alone. This feeling of being left, physically or emotionally is so intolerable that it has to be squashed. The use of violence can facilitate the maintaining or regaining of a connection. The exertion of control and abuse may occur as the punishment given to the other for 'making them feel' so vulnerable. The very fragility of these relationships is what makes them so powerful. There is no neat resolution. The re-enactment that occurs within the violent relationship may be the desire to get something from the other person that one is unlikely to ever successfully or consistently get. Affirmation, acceptance, respect or affection may be what is sought from the other person but it is unlikely to be offered. Usually, because they have such a poor sense of just what these relational responses feel like.

Conversely, using violence in a relationship may be intentionally to push the other person away. Feeling unworthy of or deceitful in receiving the affections of others can result in deliberate attempts to behave in a manner designed to have the other person abandon you. This is in order to affirm what one may already feel inside – that one is not lovable. This may also play out in the decision to leave first. This may involve a violent partner leaving before they face what they fear will inevitably happen – that they will be left.

Case example: George (58) and George (still feeling aged 10)

George came up to me during a break in a training session regarding infant- and child-led practice in the context of family violence and homelessness. George had become quite emotional and he told me how clear his memories were of his father who was a very violent man. He had left the family home when George was just ten years old. George had had intermittent contact with his father over the years. Whenever they did have contact it was always at George's initiation and he always came away feeling raw and abandoned, distressed at how little effort his father made when they did come together. His father had recently passed away after becoming quite ill. George had tried to visit his father in the hospital, hoping for some sense of closure in their relationship; however, his father had refused all visitors, denying George the chance to say goodbye.

George felt like he had a weeping wound. He was angry with himself for wanting to have contact with a man who had been such a failure as a father and sad that he was never going to hear the words he wanted to so desperately hear from his father. This was that he was proud of George and what he had achieved in his life. George felt like his father still had so much power over him despite no longer being alive. As we sat together I looked at this lovely man's face and though about what a kindly soul he seemed to be. It occurred to me that perhaps something else may have been going on for his father than wanting to punish George. I reflected with George that perhaps it was not so much that his father did not want to see him before he died, but that his father may have felt too ashamed for George to see him. George had been able to build a successful family life and honourable career for himself. It may have been too much for this elderly, unwell father to feel he deserved to see his son's face or that his son should spend any time on someone who may have felt unworthy to be his father.

Following this conversation the shift in George was palpable. Despite all the violence and disappointment George had felt at the hands of his father, he still yearned, as do most ten-year-old boys, for a relationship with his father. Whether his father deserved such an opportunity is not what kept this relational tie so potently alive for George. Whether his father did see himself as undeserving is also not relevant. What appeared to make a difference for George was the move from being stuck in relational paradox where he wanted the approval of a man he did not approve of. He was able to consider his father's world from a different perspective, and to consider himself from a different perspective. Something which did not make sense about himself now held some new meaning. The lack of resolution, or the belief that maybe one day a son may feel connected to his father, is what enabled this attachment George felt towards his father to endure. This echoes the work of people such as Virginia Goldner and her colleagues, who sought a more complex understanding of gender in determining why some heterosexual couples, in spite of violence in the relationship, persisted in staying together (Goldner *et al.* 1990).

Rigidity in thinking about gender

The ground-breaking work of the Ackerman Institute for the Family purposefully strove to move beyond stereotypes of 'men as simply abusing their power and of women as colluding in their own victimization by not leaving. This description casts men as tyrants and women as masochists, which deprives both of their humanity while simultaneously capturing a piece of the truth' (Goldner *et al.* 1990, p.343). This work is important as it did not simply see people as good or bad, or men as perpetrators and women as victims. When we speak in such absolutes to children we will very quickly shut them down. They will not trust that we can tolerate hearing about their ambivalent feelings in relation to someone who has been labelled as a perpetrator. When they have no avenue to safely make sense of their conflicting feelings of attachments to family members considered as 'bad', they risk withdrawing, feeling shamed and shameful. As we come to terms with our shared humanity, and open up to reflecting on women's use of violence and the nature of violence which exists within same sex relationships, we may come to allow ourselves new ways of thinking about how we, all of us, engage in behaviours that dominate and disadvantage others.

When we do harm by leaving children alone

The adult centric nature of family violence practice has often resulted in adding to the distress of traumatised infants and children. As workers and as carers we can unwittingly cause children further relational trauma by separating them from their strong and primary emotional attachments. This frequently occurs in extreme and high risk situations where the child is considered at imminent risk. Despite the potential risks posed in volatile situations, they can be thought through better to minimise the distress children experience. 'Ripping the Band-Aid off the wound' is not the approach I would ever advocate for the infant or small child. If a child needs to be removed, thought must be given to how this can be done with the infant's or child's emotional safety in mind. Otherwise we are only serving to further traumatise the child. We might understand why this is being done, but the child will not. We (the adults) need to find ways to 'ease the emotional pain and grief that the infant experiences in separation from the only caregiver they have known' (Jordan & Sketchley 2009, p.17) and this is helped by seeing the world from the infant's perspective.

Case example: Ally (4 years old) and Anne

A neighbour had noticed that Anne's ex-partner Sofia had begun to visit Anne and Ally's home late at night. Sofia would leave again in the early hours of the morning. The neighbour was aware that an intervention order had been taken out against Sofia because of her violence towards Anne and was worried about Ally's safety. When the neighbour heard a violent altercation in the early hours of the morning, she contacted police who visited the house and escorted Sofia from the premises. Later that morning two child protection workers arrived at Anne's doorstep with a court order to remove Ally. Both workers were unknown to Ally, and they took a frightened and wailing Ally and escorted her to court. Anne hurriedly packed some of Ally's belongings and followed behind in a taxi. Ally and Anne spent over four hours at court separated from each other. Whenever Anne heard the cry of a child in the packed waiting room in the court house she was sure it was Ally and her heart would leap. Anne was eventually called before the court and readily agreed to enter a refuge with Ally. Ally clung to her mother when reunited and during the taxi ride to the refuge and would not leave her mother's side throughout the first week of their stay.

While the circumstances of Ally's removal may have been warranted, the unexplained separation from her mother throughout this process was not. This situation was no doubt distressing for all, including for the child protection workers. However, the adults in this situation were better equipped to manage the enormity of this distress than was Ally. If a child-led perspective had been taken, some very different decisions could have been made to prevent Ally being separated from her mother. The same outcome could still have been achieved. This could have begun with Anne accompanying Ally in the child protection vehicle. Further, support could have been provided directly to both Anne and Ally together to endeavour to minimise the distress this daughter and mother were feeling during this perhaps warranted, but nevertheless highly distressing, experience. The adult centric nature of this process, which was intended to protect the child, inadvertently caused the child much distress and potential psychological harm. The irony of adult centric thinking is that it was also highly distressing for Anne and no doubt for the workers as well.

It is common practice in the family violence sector for the child/children to be separated from the parent/s when attending office-based appointments. This is particularly worrisome when the family arrives for their very first appointment. The worker/s and environment of the office are unknown to the child who is already on high alert. They may feel that such appointments are important even if they do not know or understand why. In the belief that it is better for the child not to hear their mother (or father) talk about the violence, some agencies relegate children to their children's playroom. This may or may not be with a worker accompanying them. The play space may be some way from the office where their parent is sitting or often they are placed close to or within the reception area so that administrative staff can keep an eye on them. This may sometimes be appropriate. Often it may not.

Children already distressed by exposure to violent events need to remain close to their mother/caregiver. If this is not to be in the same room, then at least make it easy for the child to get ready access to their mother (e.g., leaving the office door ajar). Notwithstanding the importance of confidentiality, services truly committed to providing family sensitive practice when dealing with family violence need to consider their physical layout from the child's perspective. How can we keep children connected with their caregivers even if we need to separate them? This might involve putting glass panelling between a playroom for the child and the office where a mother is sitting to enable visual connection. It may be that the child is shown where their mother/ caregiver is and given permission to come and knock on the door whenever they need to. As the child becomes more reassured, the less they will need to check on their caregiver. Should they not be reassured then you are being told something about the quality of their relationship, the level of trauma or both.

An expectation that older siblings will take care of younger siblings, by either the carer or the worker, misses an invaluable opportunity to see how this family system works together. Asking the children how they want an introduction to a new worker or service to work, or simply waiting and watching how they navigate who goes where and with whom, can offer invaluable insights into how this family unit operates.

The importance of siblings

Those familiar with the book or the film *A Series of Unfortunate Events, by Lemony Snicket* (by Daniel Handler) will know that it is a pretty grim tale. The three children in the story are suddenly orphaned after their parents die in a fire. The book follows a series of frightening events as an evil relative endeavours to secure their guardianship in order to inherit their parents' fortune. The story, as despairing as it is, does, however, celebrate the ingenuity of children and the ignorance and cruelty of adults. Violet (14), Klaus (12) and infant Sunny Baudelaire are the books heroes. Central to their inventiveness and tenacity is their bond with and love for one another. How often do we as adults under-estimate and underutilise the strength, hope and resilience siblings provide? This relationship can be as important as the relationship with their parents, and for some children, it is even more so. Siblings often act as pseudo-parents to their younger or even older brothers and sisters. Some do a remarkable job. The attachment formed between siblings is no less powerful than the attachment with a parent; however, this relationship can often be dismissed or simply overlooked. Once again, when 'adult centric' thinking triumphs, the feelings and attachments siblings have for one another are trivialised. Decisions regarding placements in out-of-home respite or care can, in my experience, be disastrous when sibling relationships are not considered.

Placement decisions are regularly made which attend to the immediate needs of the infant or child (singular), without consideration of what these multiple losses of attachment (parent/s and siblings) may mean in the here and now for their emotional development. Adequate and safe care notwithstanding, multiple relational losses all at once can cause harm in a way not dissimilar to exposure to violence. These multiple ruptures can be disastrous for the infant. When there is no option other than having to separate children from their siblings, then the system, or you as the child's advocate, need to work at safeguarding the next best thing. This is ensuring (and really ensuring) there is regular, unbroken contact with their siblings. Where sibling relationships may replicate damaging familial dynamics, rather than the strong protective bonds illustrated in the story of the Baudelaire children, it is our task to seek to understand what is being played out.

Each of these children will be enacting distressing emotional and relational dynamics which can be understood in the context of what they have come from. If we put our minds to understanding these relationships, they can also be supported to shift and develop in new and different ways within a context that supports where they are now (Chapter Seven will discuss working with children in groups and the family).

Making new meanings in new contexts

The arrival of a baby creates a new context for couples and families. This will be discussed in more detail in Chapter Seven. The departure of the person who is identified as violent or the act of leaving that person and moving into different accommodation or with friends or extended family also creates a new context and new opportunities for relating. Seeking out services and meeting with a worker, phoning a helpline to discuss options for leaving, or asking questions about the impacts of violence on children, all open up new possibilities for making meaning. For example, should the helpline worker ask about children, or hear the voices of children or a baby in the background, it is simple to ask, 'if your child could speak to me on the phone and tell me what it is like to live in your home when their parents are fighting, what might they tell me?' You could also ask questions such as, 'what do you see in your child's face which makes you think they feel safe? How is that different when you think they are feeling unsafe?' Or perhaps, 'when you were little did you ever feel like no one really kept you safe? Are there times when your child might feel that?'

Any questions which encourage parents to see the world from their child's perspective can open up new insights. These questions are not intended to shame parents, even if these associations are evoked. Shame is a feeling all of us are familiar with. Shame is perhaps one of our most commonly experienced emotions, but one of the least talked about because it is least liked and certainly least tolerated. Most of us will do anything to escape feeling ashamed. Yet, to work with family violence, we need to not rush to rescue others from shameful feelings but make ourselves available to stand by and support infants, children and adults to tolerate and survive the feelings of shame and the behaviours that may occur as a result. We do not need to see shameful behaviour as acceptable, but we do need to see such behaviour as understandable.

There are many opportunities for creating new meanings in a variety of settings, either when we, as workers, enter the family's context or when they enter ours. Some of these opportunities will be discussed further in Chapter Seven with specific ideas presented about what one might do in these particular contexts. The emphasis here is on the shift in us as the worker, foster carer or other caregiving adult:

> Infant/Child led work requires a shift within the mind of the therapist (or, maternal child health nurses, refuge workers, caseworkers, intake workers, child protection, lawyers, police, family support workers) and a curiosity about just what the infant/child may be thinking, imagining, expressing and feeling. Infants and children are not objects that we do things to, or passive participants in the therapeutic process who we work on, but are willing, able and available unique subjects who are communicating volumes to their external world about how their internal world is faring. (Bunston 2008a, p.335)

This shift of thinking in the mind of the other – you – leads you to bring something new to your work and to your relationships with infants, children and the whole support network that surrounds them.

SUMMARY

In infancy, and throughout our entire lives, we undertake a process of making meaning about ourselves, our relationships and the events that shape us. As we age, our ability to discover and to wonder can be blunted by what feel like the harsh realities of life. This is no more so than for someone exposed to repeated relational violence. As workers and carers, we offer an enormous amount to those we work with by providing what many of us believe are basic entitlements in life: care, support, respect, trust and emotional availability. Moreover, we can offer our minds, by providing a thoughtfulness and an ability to think with others about their meanings. We can offer infants and children, as well as their parents, a meeting of minds, offering a safe space to wonder and to discover. Discovering new meanings and imagining new possibilities are pathways to growing new parts of ourselves, and those we work with, in our quest to do more than simply survive.

Chapter Five

Whether the person you are engaging with is one month old, four years old or forty-one years old, the commitment remains the same. Whether the person is female, male or transgendered, we have all entered this world the same way. And from our earliest years we have all sought to be understood, to understand ourselves and to understand others.

Infant-Led Practice Before and Across the First Three Years

This, and the following two chapters, are concerned with 'what to do' in the room and/or in the relationship with different age groups impacted by family violence. In some ways, this section has been the easiest for me to write as it is drawn from my direct practice. However, after years of working with literally thousands of infants, children and their families, I can also see how much I still do not know, have not done and may never yet do. What may disappoint some is that what I present is not a formula. My practice experience, particularly with something as complex and as significant as family violence, is that there is no one way to work. Rigid structures and prescriptions will not meet or offer what is needed. However, the central tenets that we need to remain steadfastly committed to are:

- always keeping the infant or child safe

- always keeping the infant or child at the centre of our thinking and practice

- always accessing good reflective supervision.

It is important to arm ourselves with as much professional and theoretical knowledge as we can access and then, leaving all our assumptions at the door, begin again. Each encounter is one of coming to know the person or people we are meeting with, and together we uncover their story of what was, what is and what might yet be.

Informing this work is a proposed approach for 'thinking emotions' and the suggested use of 'guiding practice principles', as has been described in Chapter Three. This approach, as well as the practice principles, is informed by research regarding the development of the brain, and relevant theoretical thinking as explained in Chapter Two. It is important to keep in mind the important implications of exposure to relational violence on early development from birth and beyond. This is what makes our work with infants both crucial and urgent. The most significant of implications include the potential for the infant to suffer and/or experience:

- long-term negative impacts on the developing infant's regulatory systems

- sensory overload coupled with the risk of significant attachment difficulties

- risk of significant learning difficulties and other developmental delays

- mental health difficulties that may exacerbate over time.

It is important to keep these in mind, and that we offer the infants and children we work with a greater sensitivity around how we respond to them, and what we expect from them. All too often we can label children with problematic behaviours as naughty, oppositional or sullen. We may worry that they may be on the autism spectrum or have attentional problems (ADD or ADHD). It is important to consider that these little ones may be displaying evidence of significant and early childhood trauma. Regardless of what label we may want assigned to the infant and/or child, our response in treatment should remain the same: getting to know, and coming to form a working and therapeutically useful relationship with, this child and with their family. The magic of working with infants and toddlers is that they provide endless 'in the moment' opportunities to explore, with curiosity, just what is going on for them, and as it is happening within their relationship with their caregiver. However, even before they are born, we can discover something of the infant's experience.

IN UTERO

It may not be a question you have ever asked, or even considered, however, the circumstances of the conception of an infant are important. For some infants, exposure to family violence commences in utero and for some, from conception. Where your work is directly related to addressing family violence, respectfully asking a mother if the conception of their baby was consensual can open up emotionally charged but important material to gently reflect on. It may be that the mother (and/or father) dreamt of being a parent from an early age. This fantasy of becoming a parent may have been tied to a need to compensate for what that person may have felt they never had themselves. The dream of becoming a parent for the teenager or older parent sometimes represents an opportunity to finally have someone in their lives that is wholly theirs and truly loves them in a way they have never felt loved. The reality of mothering for young mothers who engage in such magical thinking can be brutally harsh and the love so desperately desired can quickly turn to resentment and regret. This is particularly the case when the father of their infant is violent and the imminent arrival of the infant stirs up both conscious and unconscious memories of their own early childhood experiences of violence. The wanted baby can also become unwanted.

In my experience, it is not uncommon to hear the relief in a mother's voice when she discloses how ambivalent she has felt about having the baby. Receiving the news that they are pregnant fills some mothers with dread, and a sense of foreboding that they will now be locked into lifetime relationship with a man they may desperately want to escape. Some women have secretly had abortions without informing their violent partners, while others have told their partners of their intention to abort the baby and have subsequently been threatened by their partners should any harm come to 'his' unborn child. This is different to a commonly held perception and often reported research finding that men who use violence respond to their partner's pregnancy by increasing their violence, move from using other forms of violence, or that pregnancy is a time when partner violence begins (Chhabra 2007; Gazmararian *et al.* 2000; Menezes-Cooper 2013). We need to come back to a position of discovery and ask questions, not assume that we know. When the conception has been non-consensual, either within the intimate relationship, a brief encounter or rape, the implications for the infant–mother relationship will be profound. The opportunity to debrief, reflect and pull together some tolerable meaning of such traumas may give both the mother and infant a chance to untether the association between the traumatic event and the infant themselves. Vital, healing therapeutic work, even after the birth of the child, can be undertaken in such circumstances (Paul 2007; Thomson-Salo 2010).

Often professionals can collect rudimentary assessment data about the pregnancy, such as, 'did the pregnancy go to term? Were there any health issues for the mother during the pregnancy? What was the delivery like?' The asking of questions for the sake of asking questions is a trap all too many professionals fall into. Really listening to and exploring the answers can reveal the ambivalence, anxiety, distress or hope the parent carried throughout the pregnancy for their child. These feelings, the imagined beliefs about what this baby may be like and what this may mean for the parent, already set the scene for the relationship to come between the infant and their parent/s. Bringing these real and imagined thoughts safely out into the open gives the parent an opportunity to ponder what impact these may have on their relationship with their infant and how this may influence the way they think about their infant and how the infant may come to think about themselves. How you ask about the experience of the infant, in utero and from birth can also introduce the parent to the idea that the infant has their own subjective experience, influenced by, but also separate to their own experience.

Case example: Felina (36)

Felina was pregnant with her fifth child and entered a women's refuge with her four children due to the escalating violence of her husband. Her husband had recently lost his job and blamed Felina for getting pregnant again at a time when they could barely make ends meet. I asked Felina if I could ask her a sensitive question, adding that if she felt any discomfort in answering to just say so and she need not answer. Felina said I could ask anything and I proceeded to ask her if the conception of this pregnancy had been consensual. Felina did not hesitate, answering, 'None of my children's conceptions have been consensual!'

Felina commented that no one had ever asked her this question before. She informed me that, despite her husband's demands for sex, her children were the best things to have come out of her marriage and that she would have had nothing to live for had she not had her children. Other women I have spoken to about the conception of their baby and their experience of the baby in utero have spoken of their baby as their saviour, and their reason to go on. For some, they hope their infant may be the motivation for their partner to change. These are heavy burdens on little shoulders. Our interest in their infant and exploration of how the mother sees their infant can help the mother put into words some of the imagined roles for, or beliefs she has about, her infant. Talking together opens the way for asking what might happen if the infant does not live up to the expectations the mother has of them. Or, of how the very small infant, just starting their own journey in life, may experience holding so much responsibility for the happiness of their parent or being given the power to change their lives. We may be able to help the parent hold on to the vitality and hope that their infant's arrival generates, while enabling the parent to give their infant the support to grow into who they might become rather than what they might need them to be.

THE NEWBORN (0–3 MONTHS)

Newborn babies possess considerable sensory and motor competencies (Brazelton & Nugent 1995; Nugent *et al.* 2007; Stern 2003). Even hours after birth infants will turn their heads towards their mother's voice in recognition. They can follow sounds and show startle responses. When placed in a crawl position they can move their head to one side and they can demonstrate muscle tone through their grip and their reflexes. Infants can shut out noise and light in order to maintain or deepen sleeping states (Als *et al.* 1977; Brazelton & Nugent 1995). Infants have been shown to be capable of mimicking the facial expressions of their parents only hours after their birth (Meltzoff & Moore 1983). Infant mental health specialists have developed specific interventions which encourage the parent to see their newborn infant's competencies and emerging personality (Brazelton & Nugent 1995). The aim is to enhance the quality of the infant–parent relationship from the outset. This involves 'helping them to see their baby as a person who wants to connect with them, by helping them to notice and reflect on the meaning of their baby's behaviour, and by helping them enjoy each other from the beginning' (Nicolson 2015, p.29).

Generally, interventions such as these have been designed to increase the parent's confidence, invite greater involvement from the father, foster healthy attachments and demonstrate to the parent/s their infant's individuality (Nugent *et al.* 2007; Paul & Thomson-Salo 2014; Thomson-Salo 2014). While family violence may or may not feature in the background lives of some parents, attending to relational violence is not generally the focus of such interventions. This may be because workers are anxious not to provoke any conflict or distress for the mother and infant. It may simply be the anxiety of not naming what many professionals would prefer not to hear as they simply do not know how to respond. It can be that professionals collude with the family, dismissing worrying clues of controlling behaviours as they do not want to see, and either do not want or do not know how to take on the burden of responding. In clear cut cases where services, police or child protection services may already be involved, family violence can result in the removal of the infant, the placement of the mother and infant in a refuge or the police or court ordered removal of the person identified as the perpetrator. Commitment to recognising the infant's subjectivity and using an infant-led perspective requires sitting with tough emotions and asking tough questions.

Case example: Nialla (1 week), Marta (21) and Jeremiah (28)

Nialla and Marta had endured a difficult labour and birth and remained in hospital while Marta recovered. Nialla and Marta were developing a lovely bond and staff were confused as to why there appeared to be occasions where Nialla was very difficult to soothe and then on other occasions she appeared to settle very quickly. They were also concerned that Nialla was not putting on weight. Jeremiah was self-employed and was able to be present during the birth and through most of this first week. Jeremiah was not present in the room when staff were attending to Nialla and Marta on this occasion. Staff were observing the lovely attachment forming between Nialla and her mother as she was feeding at her mother's breast. Jeremiah was talking loudly on his mobile as he re-entered the room. Staff noticed Nialla's body jolt when she heard Jeremiah's voice as he came through the door and she immediately stopped feeding. Nialla then started to let out shallow, rasping cries. Following this, staff began to take greater notice of what Nialla was like when her father was in the room and when he was not. It soon became apparent that Nialla became agitated in her father's presence. Allied health staff were brought in to talk with Marta alone, and with Jeramiah and Marta as a couple. It was soon revealed that Jeramiah had a history of being violent in his relationship with Marta and the decision was made to keep Marta and Nialla in the hospital until a service response could be safely co-ordinated and appropriate services contacted to work with this family unit.

This scenario is not uncommon. What was uncommon was that staff caught the opportunity to see first-hand what Nialla was telling them and that they acted on it. Had Marta not had birth complications she would have left hospital with Jeremiah only days after Nialla's birth. In the busy, bustling space of the hospital, staff may have opportunities to see infant responses that may seem incongruent, but not take notice of them. This is either because they are quickly dismissed as meaningless in those early days' post-birth or are seen but not thought about by staff as they have so many other pressing matters occupying them. It may also be that staff tend to focus on the mother/baby relationship and less so on the father.

Universal services that actively seek to engage fathers pre- and post-birth are not readily available. While services are beginning to give fathers more attention, this work tends to target fathers who already present as motivated. The secrecy and shame inherent in family violence and the public advertising campaigns that admonish domestic and family violence are predominately targeted at men. Notwithstanding the absolute need and responsibility to enforce and effectively respond to the criminality of family violence, these publicity campaigns appear to have made little impact on the numbers of family violence incidents. Perhaps the money may have been better spent on developing innovative programs to reach new and soon-to-be-fathers that are known to have used violence. Chapter Seven will detail a group work program for fathers and infants where the fathers were referred on from a men's behaviour change program.

As a worker or carer, what is important to take first and foremost from the case about Jeremiah above is a recognition that the infant possesses what Daniel Stern called an emerging self (Stern 2003). This refers to the infant's emotional and biological self that exists from birth and begins the tasks of organising sensory and relational experiences. As the infant develops, so too does the sophistication with which they sort these experiences. The three-week-old infant is very capable of giving parents very clear messages about what interests them, what frightens them, how they seek to engage with others and how they shield themselves from things they find overwhelming. It is we as adults who are often lagging in our capacity to be aware of the infant's subjectivity. The infant drinks in the world around them, eager to engage with their caregivers. What we as workers can do, and as (parents, foster or kinship) carers can respond to, is listen to the communications infants are offering us about how they feel. Even when the infant has medical concerns we must not dismiss the emotional-relational world of the infant and the intimate connection between both. When we capture what the infant is showing us in the here and now and reflect this back to the parent, we are opening up possibilities for that parent to see their infant in a new, and sometimes revelatory, light.

Case example: Stephanie (12 weeks), Tom (27) and Melissa (26)

Tom was referred into a group for mothers and fathers and their infants where the participating fathers had graduated from a men's behaviour change program. First-time parents Tom and Melissa were impressed with how their daughter Stephanie was showing her interest in the other infants in the group, particularly two siblings, male toddlers who were running around the room and who would stop now and then in front of Stephanie and talk to her. As we all began to take notice of Stephanie and her increasing delight in watching the two boys and her increasing vocalisations, Tom seemed to have a light bulb moment. He told the group about how he and Melissa were having an argument over the weekend while Stephanie was feeding at her mother's breast. Stephanie detached herself from her mother's breast and started to make noises, as if protesting. It was not until Stephanie was reassured by Melissa that they would stop fighting that Stephanie reattached to her mother's breast. Tom's eyes seemed to grow in wonder as he began to contemplate just how much Stephanie was letting them know about her world and what she liked and did not like. Much singing occurred in the group which Stephanie seemed to love. Tom, who at first said he was not a good singer and preferred not to sing in front of the group, was observed on several occasions quietly singing to Stephanie when the group was busy with other matters.

Tom was in love with his infant Stephanie and becoming more so as time went on. He was also very much in love with Melissa. However, he and Melissa had both come from backgrounds where they had experienced violence in their childhoods. He revealed just how inadequate he had felt as a partner and father and found the group experience of seeing just how much Stephanie, as well as the other infants in the room, were telling us about their worlds a revelation. His own father had been absent for much of his childhood. They had spent more time together when Tom became a young adult. Tom yearned to create a different relationship with his daughter than he had had with his father. Melissa and Tom acknowledged that they both had volatile tempers and that both had sought counselling support separately and together, to build a different future for their family than what they had experienced growing up. Their involvement in this group was one of a range of supports they had accessed to save their marriage and prepare for parenthood. It was also the beginning of their realisation that it was not just themselves, but Stephanie too, who were active participants in this new family. Stephanie also deserved to have her emotional wellbeing respected and her earliest relational experiences considered.

The motivation for parents to work on creating change for the sake of their infants must not be under-estimated. The infant represents a chance for some parents to make good on things in their lives that have not been positive to date. For the perpetrating parent/s, the birth of an infant can be the catalyst for taking steps to access assistance that they would never have dreamt of taking for themselves, or for their partner. Until we provide more innovative service responses in this critical window of opportunity, we may unwittingly reinforce the perpetual shame and secrecy that surrounds the use of violence in the beginning of many infants' lives. To wait to provide services to children when they are older ignores both the agency of the infant to contribute to growth and the damage done to them in the interim.

INFANTS (3–18 MONTHS)

The infant's emerging sense of self and their developing brain are directly shaped by their relationship with others (Cozolino 2006). Psychiatrist Daniel Stern suggests that from age two to six months infants begin to develop what he refers to as 'core relatedness', involving the capacity to see their primary caregiver as separate to themselves (Stern 2003). This is a secondary level of inter-subjectivity, which by nine months results in the infant's capacity to accurately interpret or, depending on the quality of their relationship, misinterpret the caregiver/s behaviours. The misinterpretation of a caregiver's behaviours and a poor ability to read their own internal feeling states occurs when the infant's internal world is not consistently validated by their external world. For example, should an infant see and feel frightening things, but their caregiver dismisses or contradicts their distress, the infant is left with feeling not only overwhelmed but also very confused. They feel upset but their caregiver tells them nothing is wrong or fails to come to their aid. There is an incongruence between what they feel inside and what their outside world is telling them is happening. Such a lack of congruence between what is happening for the infant and how their parent responds was evident in the case examples of Jed and Chrissy, and Clara and Shiala in Chapter Four.

This incongruence, or mismatch, can happen in any family when a parent tells their sad child to be happy or treats them like they are happy, when, clearly, they are not. However, the sheer enormity of exposure to graphic and terrifying violence has far more serious implications for the infant. This is in part because the person who frightens them may also be the person they want to go to for protection, or their protective parent may be either physically hurt or traumatised and unable to adequately respond to the infant. What makes working with the infant so important and powerful, however, is their capacity for relational repair and their desire to make good with a parent or parents, despite previous relational ruptures. Infants and young children are amazingly forgiving and tend to blame themselves over their parent/s. Furthermore, the ideas a parent carries about their child tends to be more hopeful and less rigid when the child is an infant, compared with their ideas about their older children. In my therapeutic practice with infants, mothers and fathers affected by family violence, I have seen much more rapid, positive shifts in their relationships than in my work with older children and their parents. This is, I believe, because parents tend to become more disillusioned about what their child/ren are becoming when they are acting out or having difficulties at school. They feel less competent in their parenting skills than earlier in their infant's life. Also, infants often work hard at trying to become what their parent wants them to be, as for some, it is a matter of survival.

Case example: Billy (15 months) and Tessa (32)

Billy and his mother Tessa attended a toddler/mother group for families affected by family violence. The mothers in the group started to talk about their partners and Tessa became increasingly distressed as she recalled a particularly violent incident. She spoke about how she still loved her partner but could not continue to live with him. She felt enormous sadness that the man she had believed would take care of her had let her down. As the mothers were speaking they lost sight of their infants and did not notice how quiet the five infants in the room had become. Billy had been playing a rowdy bang-the-toys-together-game with the other toddlers but as his mother was talking he had left his toys to come and stand behind her and was rubbing the top of her head. Billy then went over to another mother as she began talking and started to rub her head as well. One of the facilitators of the group drew everyone's attention to Billy and what she was observing him doing, and to how quiet all the toddlers in the room had become. She then asked the group what they made of Billy's behaviour.

The group speculated on what they believed Billy was trying to achieve: to give comfort to his mother and then to another mother in the room. As the group unpacked what they thought might be happening for Billy one of the group members spoke to Billy directly. She said, 'That's a bit tough, Billy. You having to look after Mummy when she is not feeling well?' This reflection was like a thunder-bolt through the room. Tessa grabbed Billy and said to him, 'Billy, I'm ok baby.' The mothers in the group then had a profound discussion about their infants and what the infant might worry and carry for them. They also quickly noticed the shift in the room as the infants became increasingly noisy again, and Billy brought a toy to his mother for them to bang on together.

Profound things happen in our work with infants, toddlers and children when we are open to capturing them in the moment and offering some reflections, and/or asking the caregiver/s to offer some reflections about their infant's actions and their possible meanings. When we take no notice of the infant or child, we miss them. The example above shows how the mothers in the group could consider what was happening before their very eyes, once a new set of eyes, the worker's, brought this to their attention. It is important not to state, 'Billy is obviously feeling like he has to take care of you', or 'You are encouraging your toddler to take on a parenting role when you are upset in front of him and let him comfort you'. You are carving out space to reflect. Infants will comfort their parent and this is a natural response. However, this was about making a space to think about possible meanings, not absolutes. Where you end up will vary. If you remain open, the process has the potential to be organic and unfold as discoveries are made. The meanings are made within the context of relationships. This is for the infant with their mother, and the mother with their infant. Additionally, it is with you with their infant and the infant with you, and their mother, and with all three of you together, or if in a group, a whole myriad of others.

Australian infant mental health pioneer, Ann Morgan, suggests that, 'while I am doing things with the baby I am asking the mother to think about what is going on for the baby. Mothers are often preoccupied with how they are as mothers, and I try to help them see the baby by helping them see what goes on with the baby with me' (Morgan 2007, p.14). Directly engaging with the infant does not undermine the mother or father. Nor is it intended to somehow show them how the job of parenting is done. We relate to the infant as an equal participant. By looking at and speaking to the infant, introducing ourselves and gently making their acquaintance, we demonstrate our belief that the infant is a person, in and of themselves. The infant is separate to and intimately connected with their caregiver. While honouring the subjectively of the infant, you also respect the bond between parent and infant. Perhaps you can sometimes speak for the infant, offering a possibility of putting into words what the child cannot yet say.

Case example: Clancy (6 months) and Valerie (26)

I was still relatively new in undertaking work with infants. My clients, Clancy and his mother Valerie, were about to leave after our first session together. Valerie suddenly announced that she wanted to use the bathroom. Before leaving she thrust Clancy into my arms, and she disappeared. I stood with my arms outstretched, holding Clancy under the armpits, his legs dangling. We looked at each other in shock. It was as though time slowed down as we simply stared at each other. The next thing I knew Clancy let out an almighty wail as I stood holding him, arms still stretched out, him feeling overwhelmed and me thinking, 'what do I do now?' Valerie returned, swept Clancy out of my arms, calmed him down, and was off.

I cannot count how many times this scenario has been repeated in individual work and in group work. Mothers have sometimes announced they are going, but more often have simply disappeared to use the bathroom or have a cigarette break, leaving their infant with others they barely know. The infants often unaware they have gone until they look around to find their mother's face. What has changed for me is that I talk to the infant if their mother suddenly leaves unannounced. I use my voice to try and calm them and acknowledge that it's scary when Mummy suddenly disappears. When the mother returns, I tell her what I saw happen for her infant when she suddenly left and I try and imagine what it might have been like for her infant to suddenly have their mother disappear. The conversation is not used as a guilt trip, but as recognition that whatever a mother does also has meaning for her infant. Some mothers are surprised that they are important to, and for, their baby's sense of wellbeing.

Interacting directly with the infant, talking to the infant, singing with the infant, asking the infant permission to touch their hand or to play with them sometimes offers infants a very new and potentially powerful relational experience. They may not understand what you say but they will certainly understand the intonation of your voice and the expression of your face. They will let you know if you approach them too suddenly or intrusively by averting their gaze or turning their head, or simply pulling back from you. Their body posture will tell you how comfortable they feel when being held by their parent. The overly floppy baby may seem to have given up or disappeared in their relationship with their parent. The overly rigid baby may be on hyper-alert or may feel like they have to hold themselves together as their parent cannot. How much the infant returns the gaze of their parent or averts their eyes, how the infant may jolt their body when a parent approaches or settles, gives you an enormous amount of information and material to reflect on and make sense of with the infant and with the parent. This is how we bring something new and different for them to consider in their relationship.

Case example: Torrus (9 months) and Sinneada (29)

Torrus and Sinneada enjoyed a loving relationship and it was observed by a number of group members how much they seemed to 'drink in' each other with their eyes. Torrus was clearly in love with his mother and his feelings were reciprocated. This twosome engaged in much chatter when together and Torrus would follow his mother's face and take his cues from her in any discussion or play that occurred in the group. In the last week of an eight-week group, an end-of-group celebration had been planned. The mothers brought food to share and facilitators had organised a small memento of the group for each infant and mother. Torrus and Sinneada arrived late and everyone noticed the dark purple bruising around Sinneada's right eye and cheek. After this dyad had settled into the space, one of the other mothers asked Sinneada if she was alright. Sinneada looked very sad and turned her face away from Torrus and the group and looked towards a window in the room.

Sinneada explained how her ex-partner Torren, the father of Torrus, turned up unexpectedly at their home as she was leaving with Torrus to go shopping. Torren assaulted Sinneada. It was only through the actions of a Good Samaritan walking his dog that Torren did not cause her further harm. Torrus was in his pram and saw the whole incident. Police were called by a neighbour and escorted Torren from the property and charged him with grievous bodily harm. Torrus, so used to seeing his mother's face, became increasingly distressed as he stretched his head from one side and then the other in an attempt to see his mother's face, as she was talking. When Sinneada eventually turned her face back to the group it was tearstained and Torrus seemed at a loss as to how to make sense of his mother's pain. As we gently unpacked the events that had occurred, Sinneada shared with the group that in her culture it was shameful to talk so openly about such personal feelings. Sinneada wanted to shield Torrus from her shame and could not look at him as she told her story.

In the group, and then further in a therapeutic newsletter we sent after each group (to read more about the use and examples of a therapeutic newsletter see Appendix Four) we reflected on the meaning Sinneada's turning away may have had for Torrus. In that week's newsletter we wrote:

> One of the infants seemed to be searching for his mother's face, wanting to connect with what and who are the centre of his universe. Sometimes mothers try to shield their babies from their sadness, trying to put on a happy and comforting face. It is interesting to reflect on what would give a baby more comfort, a sad and unhappy face or having no face at all to look into?

This reflection followed a profound discussion in the group about how infants need help to make sense of complex events and emotions. There was so much that occurred for Torrus and Sinneada in relation to the violent assault and its aftermath. Witnessing his father's brutality, seeing his father held down by a stranger and removed by the police. Seeing his mother's beautiful face cut and swollen. This all happened so fast and so unexpectedly, interrupting their normal and, until then, peaceful daily routine. As this event was recalled and became alive again for Torrus and Sinneada in that group work room, surrounded by safe and supportive others, this pair had a chance to revisit something that seemed senseless. Together, with others, they could begin to make meaning of something brutal and unthinking and make this somewhat less traumatic, and affirmed by the group, certainly less shameful. This particular group's ending stands out for me as a huge moment of learning. Family violence work is unpredictable. As much as we had planned for a celebratory group ending, the sober reality is that this work is messy and confronting. As much as Sinneada had planned to move on in her life with Torrus, the shadow, in this case the reality, of continued violence, remained.

TODDLERS (18 MONTHS TO THREE YEARS)

By three years of age young children clearly recognise that others have feelings and intentions that are distinct from their own, can verbalise their own and others' feelings and 'take into consideration the mental state of the other in planning and structuring of actions' (Fonagy *et al.* 1991). However, research undertaken by Coll and colleagues (1998) found that infants exposed to significant risk factors such as homelessness and violence began to fall significantly behind their normative developmental milestones at around 18 months of age compared to their peers who were not exposed to such risk factors. What this means is that what was perhaps masked by the infant's dependency on their caregiver becomes more obvious as these little ones begin to branch out and explore their social world. As infants grow into toddlers they become much more mobile, both physically and socially. This is rewarding for workers/carers and exhausting. Keeping up with toddlers is demanding and sometimes even more so when these little ones are traumatised and struggle to manage their day-to-day emotional states.

Our job as workers and/or carers is to begin where the child is at, not where we believe they should be. We need to be able to follow their lead and see what patterns may emerge to allow us some insight into what their world experience may have been to date. There is much we can learn about toddlers from our very first contacts. It became our practice in running groups to watch carefully how toddlers would enter the room from the very first week of group. This included the little ones who would rush ahead of their mothers and burst into the room without apparent fear of what lay within and those who clung to their mothers and would not release their grip even weeks into the group. How toddlers have learnt to manage stress becomes very apparent early on as they, and their carers, feel great stress in new situations.

Case example: Ashley (19 months) and Tammy (24)

Note: Apart from their names these are unaltered process notes written about a toddler and mother by facilitators directly after the first session of an eight-week infant/mother and family violence group, run a few years ago. Tammy had two children and had recently stayed in a women's refuge:

> *Arrived on time. Wendy let them into the room, then the two other facilitators entered. Ashley appeared happy and interested in others. He explored the room and attempted to connect with facilitators and other group participants through touching, this often turned to hitting or taking whatever the other person held, Tammy would say 'no' or 'gentle' in a raised and firm voice, perhaps aggressive. Ashley seemed to seek out others, Tammy not seeming to notice him, until he did something wrong. Tammy did seem angry, speaking quite loudly into her mobile phone after the group members were asked to perhaps leave phones off during group, she also held a conversation with another mother Sally whilst others in the group were talking. In the twinkle, twinkle little star, song, Tammy initially chose not to participate, having placed Ashley on the cushions. Tammy did seem to delight in seeing Ashley enjoy the song and stars, and she then knelt down next to him.*

How Ashley and Tammy presented in the first week of this group was repeated over the following weeks. Ashley appeared to use himself more than his mother to negotiate his way socially and emotionally in the group. Early on Tammy had announced to the group that Ashley was a terror. She spent what seemed to be more time talking about her other child who was not in the group than she did about Ashley. Ashley often appeared dysregulated, but also possessed a delightful and mischievous sense of humour. He was quick to engage with the facilitators and to use them to emotionally support himself when he became over-stimulated or to work through his social interactions with the other toddlers in the group. Tammy quickly assumed an influential position in the group and would show her disdain at comments or behaviours she did not agree with. She presented as aloof and in week three of the group challenged me directly asking, 'What exactly is the purpose of this group?'

As facilitators we were able to remain calm, to engage with and not dodge questions or complex discussions that arose in the group. I said that she had asked a very good question and that, 'It was about spending time together thinking about the infants.' We enjoyed Ashley immensely and he thrived in the group space. We could give him direct feedback if he pushed one of the other toddlers too hard or threw a ball at us when playing. His behaviour settled over several weeks and Tammy's cool demeanour began to thaw. We moved between reflecting on the childhood experiences these mothers had had and what they imagined their children were experiencing with them now, and how they (the toddlers) might describe their relationship with them in the future. Tammy began to capture glimpses of how others in the group experienced Ashley. She began to become curious about what Ashley thought of her and what sense he had made of being in a refuge and why they had left his father. By no means did the group, in and of itself, resolve all the traumas or disconnection this twosome demonstrated in their relationship. But it did give Tammy a 'good enough' therapeutic experience to choose to go on and undertake further work with both sons and herself. Ashley's capacity to so quickly change in the group space gave Tammy enough evidence that this 'talking and playing stuff' made a difference for one son and she was prepared to commit to long-term family work for herself and her children.

As described in Chapter One, every contact counts. Every worker (or foster or kinship carers) can contribute individually to making a difference in the lives of the children and families we work with. Ashley and Tammy had experienced 'good enough' relational encounters with refuge workers to take the next step of joining a therapeutic group program. The group work experience gave Ashley and Tammy enough confidence to not only move onto family work but to remain working with the one therapist for nearly two years. I and my fellow group facilitators were not that certain that Tammy (out of all the mothers who attended) would return to the group after week one. Tammy had been the hardest mother to engage and the most difficult to read. I suspect she returned for Ashley rather than for herself. Tammy and Ashley came even after Tammy had had a minor medical procedure two days before. Ashley showed us what he wanted from us as facilitators and from the group itself. He wanted intimacy and he wanted to be enjoyed. So too did Tammy, but unlike Ashley, she was less confident, and more hardened from a life of family violence and disappointment, to ask for it.

Case example: Markus (30 months) and Marylyn (29)

Following their attendance at a toddler/mother group work family violence program, Markus and Marylyn were referred to me for some individual work. Markus had been very difficult to manage in the group and was aggressive towards the other children. His mother was very apologetic but appeared to have few strategies to manage his behaviour. On several occasions one of the facilitators took Markus out of the group with his mother to calm him down, but as soon as they returned to the room he would again quickly spiral out of control. Markus, Marylyn, Marylyn's aunty and one of the group facilitators attended the very first session. We needed to use a different office to the one I occupied as maintenance work was being undertaken and I used a colleague's office in the same corridor. When the family arrived, Markus entered the room and sat next to his mother on a couch. Markus made no eye contact and did not respond to me when I said hello and he began fidgeting through his mother's handbag. I watched him while the adults spoke and noticed that when the subject of his father came up he stopped fidgeting. As his mother gave a potted history of the violence she and Markus had experienced Markus jumped from the couch and went to the light switch next to the office door. He proceeded to flick the switch on and off repeatedly, much to the embarrassment of his mother and great-aunty. He was doing no harm. I suggested we not intervene and perhaps it might be that Markus was trying to tell us something.

Markus soon tired of the light switch and then grappled with and finally successfully opened the office door. To his delight and my dismay, the office door opposite was open. This room was like Aladdin's Cave. The worker had every sort of toy, action figurine and children's game you could imagine, with wall shelves and bookcases crammed full. I quickly moved into gear and followed him, talking with him about each discovery as he found one thing after the other after the other. I eventually suggested he choose three things to take back into 'our' other office and with some help to accomplish this we both returned to the room. This family had a complex history of substance use, family violence and mental illness. I continued to see Markus and Marylyn for 14 months and referred them on to another worker when they secured housing in another region. Every time Markus saw me he wanted to revisit Aladdin's Cave. Every time I said no, and explained that this was not my room but that I did have the three toys he selected on his first visit and a small number of others which we used each visit. I moved into a more spacious room from then on, which had less distractions, and in addition to the three toys he would also bring in whatever toy he wanted from home.

Markus was a great teacher. He taught me to recognise when he felt relationally overloaded, when he felt anxious, when he could not cope with too much sensory stimulation, what calmed him and what dysregulated him. Neither parent had been very available to him when he was born. They were struggling with their own lives and it appeared Markus was left flailing on numerous occasions. While both loved him and they as parents grew over time, making decisions based on what was best for Markus occurred late in his development as an infant and left him with ongoing sensory difficulties. Markus would easily become relationally and emotionally overwhelmed. When he was not coping, he would let the world know, as he demonstrated in the infant/mother group. This was not 'naughty behaviour', but reflected Markus's inability to manage when too much was happening around him, and was the result of what he was feeling internally. We worked on slowing his world down, minimising noise and distractions and giving Markus and his mother space to play together and reflect together. Markus's father no longer lived with them but had made some steps to address his violence and other issues in order to have access visits with his son.

Over the 14 months I worked with Markus he asked each time to return to the Aladdin's Cave he discovered that very first week he met me. This was despite being in that room only once and for less than ten minutes. In my work with infants and toddlers, they will invariably return to playing a particular game or use a certain toy the next time we meet. Infants and toddlers remember. When placed back in the same space, a similar space with similar objects, or a similar relational situation infants can recall and re-engage with the experience associated with pleasurable events, and traumatic ones. 'Neuroception' is a response that is not conscious, and is what Porges (2015) describes as a 'neural process, distinct from perception and sensation, capable of distinguishing environmental (and visceral) features that are safe, dangerous or life-threatening' (p.119). As discussed in Chapter Two, early trauma memories live on in the body. When working with toddlers and older children impacted by family violence it can be useful to consider that sometimes problematic behaviours, such as hitting out, or throwing and breaking things may have much more to do with their 'physiologically vulnerable states', and that when we endeavour to engage with them, they 'might misinterpret the social cues of others as aggressive' (Porges 2015, p.120). This includes other concerning presentations I have encountered regularly in this work, such as a young child who may soil themselves, or wet their pants. Once again, such behaviours are likely to be showing us how their little bodies, from an early age, and as an automatic response, would shut down in the face of overwhelming fear. Very little may need to occur for them to quickly return to a bodily response which shuts down in anticipation of impending danger.

SUMMARY

When we allow ourselves 'not to presume to know', and to be open to learning from the infants and young children we work with, we may find entry points which enable us to join with helping them in growing their sense of wellbeing in the world. Their caregiving world, whether that be their parent/s, foster carers or kinship carers, may then experience something new through reaching a deeper understanding of and curiosity about the infant/child and their relationship with them. Appreciating the inter-connectedness of the circumstances of the parent/s' world before and/or from the moment of their infant's conception through to their birth and beyond enlarges the possibilities for understanding how meaning has been made of, for and with their infant. Actively and equally involving the infant and toddler throughout each contact we have as a worker can enhance the possibility that, outside of their work with us, the infant and their caregiving world will become increasingly engaged in seeking to understand and begin to make new meanings together.

Chapter Six

Play should be the treasured companion of childhood.

Sadly, when family violence is present in the home, the pleasure found in play is often an early casualty. When things go well, dynamic, imaginative and symbolic play flourishes in a safe place wherein discovery, self-mastery and problem solving can thrive. Play is restorative and energising. It also allows for complex feelings and difficult dilemmas to be broken down into manageable pieces and sorted through; and when needed, invited or offered, the caregiver is there at the ready, and can join in with that magical realm of imagination.

Child-Led Practice and the Significance of Playfulness in Childhood and Beyond

As the child grows and changes so too must our strategies for engaging them. The principles behind our work do not change but, developmentally, progress is made and some children will want, require or demand that we move alongside them in the more sophisticated application of activities that we utilise. This can involve the use of crayons, paints, music, games, dolls, toys and a wide array of imaginative possibilities. It also helps us to become familiar with what they are interested in. What films, action figures, television shows or even computer games they favour, and to think about what it is about such preferences that has meaning for them. Making the mind-space or foster care home inviting and child-friendly is something few professional workplaces have mastered. Even when those workplaces exist to work directly with children.

Child protection services, children's courts, and child and adolescent mental health services are often those environments which are unimaginative, intimidating and unwelcoming of children. This is not solely due to the decor. The dour faces or hushed tones of busy adult faces at work can scare other adults, let alone children. Even when specific 'children's rooms', or staff members' offices are set up with children in mind, walking through a maze of corridors to get to, or to leave these spaces can be a daunting journey for young children. As we grow older we can lose touch with the seriousness of play. We simply keep the seriousness. The ability to have fun safely, and to harness the healing properties of humour and spontaneity, is sorely lacking in many family-based workplaces. This is no more so than in responding to the impacts of family violence where the very need for play is critical in helping children and adults heal. Family violence work is to be taken seriously, but it must not exclude the importance of pleasure, imagination and laughter.

RECOGNISING THE IMPORTANCE OF PLAY

Vital in this work is creating an environment where safe play can occur, for infants, children and adults alike. The capacity to play is crucial in understanding and working with children, young people and their caregivers. Infants play primarily through sensory exploration such as touch and taste, but they discover very early the inherent pleasure in play. Peek a boo games, blowing raspberries, singing and smiling games can all engage the infant in giddy delight. Even when the parent is reticent about play, the introduction of playfulness in how we relate to the infants and parents that we work with can prove highly effective in reducing anxiety and defensiveness, and can increase relational energy.

Play provides children with an intermediary space within which to explore what is going on between their internal and external world. Play is important in how the brain stores memory, develops organisational skills and extends our vocabulary. 'In our processing of information, we must not only organise it in logical structures but also examine the alternative and future possibilities or even consider the darker alternatives that appear in any human experience' (Singer 2002, p.253). Play enhances our capacity for reflecting on both positive and negative feelings; it helps with abstract thinking and enhances creative problem solving. Play offers the space in which the sense of self emerges and, as we develop in life, ushers in what is known as our 'introspective consciousness'

(Meares 1993). That is, our ability to know that we exist as an autonomous self, and that there exists a boundary between our inner world and outer world. It also facilitates coming to know that there is a duality within ourselves. It is within this space that 'symbolic play takes place in a curious atmosphere in which magic mingles with reality' (Meares 1993, p.37). This duality refers to our ability to take our experience of relating well enough to our caregivers into our internal subjective world. As we grow we learn to 'talk to ourselves'. We have an internal dialogue where we play things out in our minds; we imagine, we daydream and we reflect and sort through our thoughts about ourselves within ourselves: 'to the thoughts and images that arise when attention drifts away from external tasks and perceptual input toward a more private, internal stream of consciousness' (McMillan, Kaufman & Singer 2013, p.1).

Play is integral to healthy development. It has the capacity to be restorative, creative and explorative. Healthy play uses imagination and symbolism, which involves the ability to pretend, and to play out or work through dilemmas. Play can provide a safe place to try and make sense of things and can offer an enjoyment of self and of others. Where infants, children and young people have been severely traumatised, the opportunity to be enjoyed by others and/or to enjoy others may be severely compromised. This then impacts on how they enjoy themselves or make sense of who they are. They may become muddled about what is joyful, pleasurable reverie (or daydreaming). Traumatised children may engage in repetitive play which re-enacts rather than releases the trauma. They may become stuck, playing out a scenario that never resolves itself. As an observer, this play is distressing to watch. It may be hidden, induce embarrassment or shame in the child, or result in destructive or uncomfortable re-enactments. Such play is often unsophisticated, imprecise and difficult to make sense of. This is explained by infant mental health specialist Arietta Slade (1994):

> With children who cannot play coherently or meaningfully, who cannot use the symbols of play and language to make sense of their emotional experiences, who cannot create narratives of their experiences, an essential and prior part of the work of treatment is to help them do so...the process of playing itself is consolidating and integrative. (pp.81–82)

As workers and carers, our role is to be sensitive to the need to provide a relationally safe play space. This may be to help a child to learn how to play. While props can help, this is not about having the perfect toys, playroom, sand tray table, doll's house or play mats. We offer ourselves. We provide a relational boundary that holds them as they sort through what they feel, they imagine and they experience. This is about being with, and not about taking over, their play. We are simply there as they need us. We are a boundary that they may not have previously had, and where our presence holds them as they dip in and out of their own personal and internal 'streams of consciousness'. We do this to aid their sensory integration, 'I feel this when I do that', and offer new understanding of their experience. 'Perhaps my mum yelled at me because she was frightened, not because I am bad.' Infants need more than their basic needs met. They want to be enjoyed. When they are not engaged with, they may make sense of this as something they have done wrong, or because of something they lack (Trevarthen 2001). As they grow, these negative appraisals of self also grow, or become fixed.

THE SMALL CHILD (3–5 YEARS)

The age differentiations I have selected for this and the previous chapter make use of the biological markers we commonly use to measure the age of children and our narrative about their development. Psychological trauma work is not bound by age but inter-subjective experience. Stops and starts, or ongoing disruptions, in the internal development in the interpersonal world of children produce different consequences. As stated before, our job is to explore and discover. Ideally, the work we undertake with infants, toddlers and very young children is within the context of their caregiving environment. This means keeping their parent/s and or caregiver either in the room (or physically nearby), and actively involved. We may have occasions where we have no choice but to work with the child alone. This may be due to circumstances such as a parent is in jail or when a parent/s has died and/or has been murdered. It may be because the parent or carer is so emotionally unavailable, violent or sabotaging that the child needs, demands or deserves time away. Thoughtful consideration of whether there is a role for child protection is then necessary.

As noted in previous chapters, the youngest person in the system often holds the most hope. A small child may exhibit more pronounced and concerning behaviours than the toddler or the infant, but generally they are still innately curious and less defensive than older children. Workers often fear small children as their behaviour can seem more erratic and less understandable. Workers can assume that young children are less open to seeing reason and more likely to tantrum or misbehave. The shift in power may feel greatest around this age range as the small child acting out might leave the adult feeling powerless as they kick, scream, run away, behave with defiance or engage in behaviours that alarm or disappoint. The toddler becomes the small person who now starts to expresses their preferences, both physically and vocally. They may lose some of their babyish looks and trigger anxieties in the parent about what and who they are or may grow into.

Case example: Ajay (4), Joss (6), Mary (32) and Stephen (37)

Ajay and Joss had been exposed to significant violence by Stephen towards Mary in their early years. Mary left Stephen and Stephen sought help from a local agency to address his violence. He had undertaken both individual and group work and after a separation of some six months they reunited. Stephen remained committed to attending his men's group and Mary felt that their relationship had changed dramatically. She did, however, feel concerned about Stephen's impatience with the children, principally Ajay. They committed to some family work and it became quickly apparent that both children would go to Mary for their emotional and physical needs and Stephen remained somewhat on the periphery of this family unit. Neither Mary nor Stephen were particularly playful with the children or each other. The children would play happily enough with each other until they had to share something they both wanted. As Joss was bigger she usually won out and Ajay would collapse, and run crying to his mother. Stephen would almost physically recoil as this sight and tell Ajay off and to stop being a sook.

I reflected on the patterns I saw operating in this family and asked Stephen directly what it felt like to see Ajay run to his mother for comfort. Stephen said it felt embarrassing and frustrated him. Ajay watched his father intently as I asked Stephen questions around who he went to for comfort when he was a little boy. With some gentle probing,

Stephen revealed the story of his father who revelled in humiliating him. He would always go to his mother for support, but usually when his father was not around as his father would punish him if he showed any weakness. In reflecting on his current adult relationship with his father, Stephen still felt estranged from him and felt contempt as his father aged, becoming frailer and more emotionally demanding. This conversation created an enormous shift in the family dynamic with Stephen making very conscious attempts to offer Ajay help with doing up his shoelaces and even offering to dry him off after bath time. Ajay began to feel safe enough to reciprocate. In one of our final sessions he showed his dad how to play when the two played at racing their toy cars together. Stephen had accidently crashed his car and Ajay came up to him and patted his shoulder saying, 'It's ok, Dad, it's only pretend.'

Young children, in their play, behaviour, drawings and chatter, offer multiple entry points for reflecting in the 'here and now' about the here and now, about the past and about the future. It is not too difficult to slide back and forward in time visiting moments, emotions and dynamics that are current for the child, for the child/ parent or child/sibling relationships which act almost as a portal to other dimensions. As noted at the very beginning of this book, I believe infant- and child-led work is 'right brain' work. It is not what is thought or stated that holds resonance as much as what is felt and experienced, or re-experienced. The emotional self of the infant or child is forming right before our eyes. The child is very responsive to their environment and much quicker to notice and respond to change than is the parent. This is not some magic trick, however, this work remains steadfastly committed to the baseline as presented in Chapter Three. The starting point is what the young child requires to be safe, both emotionally and physically, and we move from the child up, not the parent down. This is again why seeing the child within their caregiving environment is so important.

Stephen needed to get his act together regarding how he treated his son. Telling him to 'get his act together' would not have succeeded. Mary had expressed her concern to Stephen about the way he treated Ajay, but it was as if he could not bring himself to feel affection for his son nor tolerate his son displaying any signs of emotion. The block, as I experienced it, was not cognitive, but more primitive and physiological. It felt distressing for Stephen to witness his young son re-enacting what he felt about his own feeling states. From Stephen's account of his own childhood, this was likely deeply entrenched feelings of shame and disapproval. Ajay brought all this evocative and potent material right into the room. As Stephen moved to see himself as a frightened little boy, and express his disappointment and anger with his father, he was also able to see Ajay as not a sook, but a little boy who wanted, needed and was entitled to reassurance. As Ajay felt reassured and affirmed in his emotional responses he became more assured and more confident within himself and his relationship with his father.

Case example: Anika (2), Terry (4½) and Shirley (31)

Terry, Anika and Shirley were in the second week of their stay at a women's refuge. Shirley appeared to be very depressed and unresponsive to her children. The staff were concerned about her mental state and general lethargy. The children were thrilled when the children's worker was on duty as they could then use the purpose-built playroom which otherwise was off-limits without adult supervision. I was visiting on a day the children's worker was not on duty and I asked if I might accompany the children into the playroom. Terry was like a whirly-bird, and seemed unable to settle with any one activity for very long. Anika sidled up beside me and seemed to enjoy the proximity over any play. I could see Shirley sitting outside having a cigarette and occasionally looking in our direction but mostly lost in thought. A relief worker had accompanied us into the playroom and sat for a short while before announcing that she should get back inside and do some work. Clearly the worker believed that, for her, 'playing with children' was not work.

The playroom was bursting with all sorts of colours, toys and exciting possibilities which seemed to overwhelm rather than stimulate Terry. I cleared some space at a table and started to cut out pieces of fabric. I had noticed that Terry had an action figure in his hand which he held on to as he went from one thing to another. As this appeared to be the one constant thing Terry had attached to, I began to ask Terry questions about this action figure. At first Terry looked at me incredulously, as if dumbfounded that I did not simply know that this was a certain 'well-known' action hero. I asked questions about the action figure's name, how he got that name, where he lived and what he did. Terry slowly settled and began to excitedly tell me all about his action hero.

As I wondered if the action hero ever got cold (as the action figure had only a lycra body suit on) Terry laughed and told me not to be silly, as he had superpowers and did not get cold. I told him that, nevertheless, I would like to make him a coat, just in case he did sometimes feel cold, or just bored with having to wear the same clothes every single day. I asked Terry if I could take his action figure's measurements and he slowly let me hold his action figure and settled down beside me, watching in fascination as I made a very wonky, uneven and ill-fitting felt cloak stuck together with fabric glue and staples.

During this cloak-making, Terry began to cut out fabric to make his action figure some pants and a hat. Anika worked busily alongside us to make her doll some dresses. Shirley popped her head in during this time just to check that the children weren't being a bother. I invited her in and asked her to sit down with us as the table. Despite hesitating, she politely accepted my invitation and she slowly joined in the play as the children excitedly explained what they were doing, why, and offered her other some jobs to do in cutting and gluing. In that short thirty-minute space with Shirley in the room I learnt an enormous amount about this family unit, what they had been through and how dysregulated they had felt following a very dramatic departure from their family home. I also saw Shirley come alive, and with her children's help, begin to play.

Terry was very literal in his play and did not seem to find pleasure, nor was he soothed by playing. He could not play, despite trying, as he instead buzzed around the playroom and was unable to settle. He did not appear able to manage his emotional states on his own, but was able to do this with some assistance. Despite his initial dismay at my suggestion that his action hero could feel the cold, he quite quickly joined in the play with my input. The play space became industrious and companionable as we all worked towards shared goals. Together we offered something nurturing to our imaginary friends, the super hero and Anika's doll. Shirley popping in to check on her children was fortuitous. It would have been very easy to reassure Shirley that we were ok and allow her to take a rest from them. It is common practice in many settings to offer mothers or parents a rest from their children. This accommodates a belief that children are energy-taking rather than energy-giving. Further, the practice of having allocated children's workers, over an expectation that all workers need to be open to respond to infants and children, reaffirms a false divide.

The real work rests in supporting families to be families. It does not rest with going off to enter data, tidy up, make appointments for families or attend to the mother. This means harnessing the energy-giving aspects of family relationships. Often these families have been robbed of this by needing to defend themselves from violence. This is not diminishing the importance of court, medical or housing appointments. But it is suggesting a re-prioritising of what is important and what is less so. Supporting relational healing through the workers themselves spending time with families doing family activities and play must not be considered side, non-work activity. These are critical activities that developmentally matter and which need to be treated and experienced relationally as mattering.

Children often have energy to spare. I have yet to find a word or phrase which captures with accuracy the beautiful feeling one has when sitting alongside a child and watching them play with industry and total concentration. You are part of the play in that they allow you to witness this truly intimate space, but you are also separate to the play. The child comes out of their reverie only enough to check you are still there or to use you momentarily and then they re-enter their magical world where they are busy sorting, creating and imagining. This being together sensation is brimming with a peaceful yet powerful energy. Spontaneous laughter and play is something children want to repeat, repeatedly. When adults truly enter this space, they too want to prolong the magic. It may sometimes be fleeting but its power revives and lifts. These are the healing moments we want to offer the infants, children and families we work with.

THE SCHOOL-READY CHILD (5+)

Children around the age of five are considered 'school-ready'. They move from the more supported, and sometimes smaller sized groupings of pre-school and other forms of child care, or straight from home, into the school system. This setting poses challenges for many small children, not the least of which is negotiating the rules of the classroom and the politics of the playground. Many pre-schools and primary schools are under-staffed and under-supported to manage difficult behaviours resulting from a family home where there is violence. It is time for such services to start advocating for increased support and training and interventions from family violence services and child and adolescent mental health, both in the school context and within pre-school services. The shift lies within how we the adult see the child, rather than the usual expectation that the child should behave in certain ways.

These young children often behave in a certain way and come with a story, usually hidden and largely unprocessed. They show us their disorganisation, inability to settle themselves or to stay on task. Learning or speech difficulties, perhaps already evident before they reach school, become more pronounced at school. Not every child who experiences family violence in the home will falter at school. Some thrive. Pre-school and primary school settings can be the second family and the difference between a child finding something positive and special within themselves and this not happening but reinforcing the reverse. Further still, not all violent home experiences fully negate the positive and protective factors that may operate in the relationships that infants and children have with their non-offending parent or other adults, or other siblings in their lives; nor the impact that leaving a violent relationship might have (Anderson, Renner & Danis 2012; Letourneau *et al.* 2013). Some infants and children have within themselves capacities which provide some internal resilience or offer their caregiving environment healing and growth (Martinez-Torteya *et al.* 2009; Masten 2011). Our focus is, however, on when restoration and resilience has floundered.

Case example: Tenielle (6), Martina (38) and Thomas (42)

Tenielle and her father had left Tenielle's mother, Sandra, after she was admitted to as a patient for treatment for her mental illness, following threats to harm both Tenielle and Thomas. Thomas and Sandra had met in their mid-thirties; both had been previously married and neither had any children. The couple were surprised when they learnt Sandra had fallen pregnant and as she was approaching her 40th birthday. They decided, with some trepidation, to proceed with the pregnancy. Sandra struggled with significant post-natal depression. The marriage, as described by Thomas, became tumultuous. Thomas was aware that

Sandra struggled in her role as a parent but did not suspect that she would ever harm Tenielle. Arriving home early from work one day, he heard splashing and walked in to the bathroom to find Sandra holding Tenielle, aged three, under the water. Sandra told Thomas she had blanked out and had no memory of what he said he had walked in on. Thomas sought help and Sandra was allocated a mental health worker by the local community mental health service.

Over the next 12 months Thomas described Sandra as becoming increasingly volatile and emotionally abusive. Following her threats to harm both him and Tenielle, Thomas separated from Sandra. Ten months later he met Martina who had adult children who now lived away from home. Sandra had little contact with Tenielle and for six months had refused to see her. Martina moved in with Tenielle and Thomas and took on a caring role with Tenielle. Tenielle found it difficult to make friends in her first year at school and was often in trouble for stealing. The school had tried many strategies to manage Tenielle's behaviour but Martina, who would search her school bag each night, continued to find pencils, books and toys that either belonged to the school or other children. I met with Tenielle and Martina as Thomas was working. Sadly, despite numerous efforts to engage him, he was only ever able to attend one session. Martina seemed to be the dominant person within their relationship and she felt that Thomas could not afford to take time off work when she, Martina, was now willing and able to take responsibility for Tenielle's care. So much had happened in Tenielle's life to date. Tenielle's compulsion to steal things seemed to provide her with some sense of compensation and control, albeit fleetingly, in a life where she appeared to have little experience of either.

Martina was quite rigid in her thinking, and although not unkind to Tenielle, offered her little nurturing. She found it difficult to consider that Tenielle's stealing might suggest something about how her empty her internal world may have felt. I suggested ongoing individual work with Tenielle, offering her something that was just hers. I met with the school. Tenielle's teacher was very gentle and thoughtful. She had not been aware of the full extent of the trauma and loss Tenielle had endured. She was quick to come up with strategies that might boost Tenielle's self-esteem and enable her to undertake some special roles such as class monitor. The school could ensure that Tenielle remained with the same teacher the following year as she was in a composite year one and two class. I remained working with Tenielle and she made much use of the doll's house. I checked in regularly with the school and over time could encourage Martina to have time-out for herself by sending Thomas and Tenielle off to do shopping chores or go to the occasional movie.

Tenielle was left with enormous grief over losing her mother, and guilt over what she believed she must have done for her mother to have left her. She had no conscious memory of her mother attempting to drown her in the bath, but, in her doll's house play she would often place the bath tub in the rooms, such as the kitchen and lounge room, where she would congregate all the (20) dolls of the doll's house. Perhaps this was her way of keeping the bathtub under constant surveillance? There may have been much that happened to Tenielle in her first years while she was alone in her mother's care which she could not consciously remember nor verbally express. It seemed important to not interpret anything in Tenielle's play, but simply to make a safe space for her to play. Over time her play expanded and she began to use imagination and take pleasure from stories she made up. She could also incorporate the not so nice aspects in her play, such as cramming a doll called Martha into the chimney head first, and invite me in to share her play when she began to feel overwhelmed. The capacities she did have in playing suggested that she carried some benevolent and positive experiences from her early caregiving with her mother and father. These positive aspects were as important to recognise and affirm, as it was to tolerate and make sense of those which were less so (Lieberman *et al.* 2005).

Tenielle called her sessions with me her 'special time' and this phrase was also picked up by Martina, Thomas and the school. Her mother, Sandra, did not resume contact but would send cards or phone on her birthday or Christmas. This scarcity of contact served as an ongoing weeping wound. Sometimes Tenielle would dictate while I wrote out a letter that was addressed to her mother but which we did not send, and which I kept for her. Martina remained somewhat undemonstrative with Tenielle, but supported regular sessions with me and in her own way proved a more consistent and reliable caregiver than her mother could be. I concentrated my work with the most receptive parts of Tenielle's world: Tenielle herself and the school. The school did not make a fuss when Martina brought back property found in Tenielle's school bag that was not hers. Her stealing reduced significantly and generally seemed to reappear when Tenielle appeared stressed by social dynamics in the classroom. Tenielle's father would generally spend time alone with Tenielle at least once a fortnight. While Tenielle would dearly have loved more than this, Thomas did keep this time as a regular commitment in his busy work schedule.

Although Tenielle continued to lag behind her peers academically, she appeared to find some emotional restoration. She made good use of the safe space provided where she was supported in her play and could talk freely and with support about her ambivalent feelings about her mother, stepmother and father. The school setting became a large protective factor, with staff managing her behavioural difficulties with great sensitivity. They ensured Tenielle had continuity in staffing and gradually and creatively transitioned her when swapping her to a new teacher and classroom at the beginning of her third year. They also helped to protect friendships Tenielle had formed with other children at school and assigned her a mentor from a higher class. Had Tenielle been much younger, I fear her context, with Thomas and Martina as parents and without the school, would have perhaps been insufficient in providing her with enough additional emotional resources to offer adequate healing. Tenielle was kept safe with her father and stepmother, but needed more to assist with healing. She was enjoyed, and kept in mind, by her teachers and me as we endeavoured to understand just what this little girl had been through and still struggled with.

Ideally, infancy, rather than later in childhood, is a time when we begin to learn about the gambit of emotions through our relationship with others, primarily our family. According to Trevarthen (2001) we are born ready to begin this learning but how this occurs depends on how we:

> adopt both imitative and complementary habits of self-expression in relation to our principal companions or mentors. But, these acquired characteristics of personality are modifications of a universal human need to be in relationships that are qualified by feelings of pride and shame, love and hate, celebrating and grieving, triumph and despair...the individual's learning of how to be a person in relation to others, with a character and emotionally valued beliefs, knowledge and skills. (pp.111–112)

Where this has stalled in infancy, as appeared to be the case with Tenielle, there was much not only to catch up on but it also left a potential emptiness that may always haunt her. Tenielle may feel compelled to find ways, either positive or negative, to keep these frightening feelings of emptiness at bay. The earlier this repair work can happen the better. However, it is never too late to bring some healing into the lives of not just children, but their parents as well.

Case example: Susie (4), Joshie (5) and Arnold (29)

Susie and Joshie had been referred into a therapeutic group for children with their father who had been through a men's behaviour change program. Arnold was the primary caregiver of the two children and during the home visit to undertake the assessment for the group, the two children ran wild. Arnold would yell at the children with little effect. Arnold had been referred to the men's behaviour change group because of his anger towards his wife's nearly adult son from an earlier marriage. This little brother and sister were very rough with one another within the group itself and would occasionally try to engage Arnold, but tended to approach him only for help with more routine tasks (like help with tying their shoelaces). Arnold revealed a very complex history of early exposure to abuse, violence and neglect. It was only in his teens when he moved in with extended family that he felt like he had found a safe home. Arnold was rather abrasive in the group and just as Susie and Joshie struggled socially in the group, so too did Arnold.

Arnold found it difficult to reflect on what might be being expressed in his children's behaviour or to offer more than cynicism about relationships and the world in general. The boisterous behaviour of both Susie and Joshie would occasionally result in them falling over or somehow hurting themselves. They never cried or asked for comfort and exhibited an astounding tolerance for pain. Susie and Joshie were the first to initiate and play games that involved rough and tumble. They loved hanging onto facilitators who, following their lead, made up a game using the floor cushions we all sat on. We made some rules to keep all six children in the group safe and this game was played, at the children's request, each week. The continuity of the play began to build social bridges for Susie and Joshie when all the children together excitedly began adding different aspects to the game. Arnold did not join any games but sat back and watched proceedings. However, in week five of our eight-week group we all heard him laugh, for the first time, as his children played the cushion game. It was as if magic dust had been sprinkled in the room. The children ran to him and asked him to join in. But they needed back-up. The facilitators pushed the cushions over to where Arnold was sitting and he eventually succumbed and joined in.

I cannot capture in words just how huge it was for Arnold to join in the group play, or what this meant for his children. Arnold had now been initiated into the group and his children thereafter ensured he was involved in all the games played in the group. This ritual involved the children needing to ask him to participate but he would now reciprocate. The change for this little family unit began with the children, both as his incentive to take the risk in joining a group to enhance his parenting, and through the attachment he had towards his children and his eventual spontaneous enjoyment of their play. Susie and Joshie's play had been chaotic, fragmented and exhausting both to watch and engage with. They were, within the group context, able to join with the rhythm of the group play relatively quickly and to find pleasure and purpose in this collective play. Their pleasure at this discovery of mutuality in play was infectious. Their joy was contagious, triggering a response in Arnold that over time by-passed his usual defensiveness and opened an opportunity that the group could quickly capitalise on. This shift, from my perspective, was remarkable. The group could move past reacting to Arnold's brittleness and discover what was childlike as well as likeable in Arnold. Susie and Joshie also found companionship with their father.

While it is not the intention of this case example to suggest that it is the role of children to unleash the child within their parent, this is, in effect, what happened for this family. Arnold had never felt safe enough to be a child during his own childhood, but was open to trusting his children in allowing a little of this repair work to happen for all of them through joining their play. Like most four- and five-year-olds, Susie and Joshie were far from being able to engage through simply talking. While some of the children we work with or care for may be both able and ready to express themselves verbally, my experience is that, in general, children who have experienced significant family violence have not learnt to understand the feelings in their internal world, let alone know how to talk about them. Whatever their age, child or adult, we have to start at the beginning, and together commit to discovering.

WORKING WITH PARENTS

I believe that, aside from the fundamental safety baseline that needs establishing, as described in Chapter Three, there are four basic goals in undertaking infant- and child-led work with parents who are either the perpetrators of and/or have experienced family violence:

- to enable the parent to become 'unstuck' in thinking what is 'stuck' about their child as well as themselves in relation to their child

- to bring their infant and/or child alive in their minds and in their interactions with their child, through experiencing their child as a person in and of themselves, separate to, but intimately dependent on and connected to them, their parent

- to make links between the present, past and future through exploring how the parent's experience of being parented themselves in the past is re-enacted in how they parent now, and by talking about how what is done now will influence their child, and their relationship with their child (and potential grandchildren) in the future

- to enable the parent to find strategies to reflect on how they block their thinking in relation to their child and their relationship, and what they, together with their child, might do to build new pathways for thinking, being and playing together.

Becoming unstuck

This approach to parent work can act as the catalyst for unlocking something that has stalled within the internal world of the adult. This is to say that parents who have been exposed to their own early, and/or the inter-generational transmission of, family violence may find that something within themselves loosens when they see or experience a direct change in their child. This occurs through working with the infant or child and their parent together, unlike in Tenielle's case above, where her father and stepmother appeared neither emotionally available nor necessarily motivated to undertake such work. Working with the infant and/or child in the room, where they are the most available and hungry for connection, can ameliorate those circumstances where:

> in some cases the parents' thinking is stuck. It may then be that, if there is change in the infant, change can come about more quickly for the parents; when we do something relieving with her infant the mother in turn feels mothered and a good internal object can be experienced again. (Thomson-Salo *et al.* 1999, p.52)

Bringing the infant's subjectivity alive

Enlivening the subjectivity of the infant occurs through both engaging directly with the child, and bringing the communications of the child to the parent's attention. Infants and children will provide you with an abundance of data to use directly in your work with their parents. Once you become more comfortable in allowing yourself to watch and reflect in the space and begin to see things happen, you can use even the simplest of observations to offer parents new possibilities for making meanings. I was interviewing a new mother in a women's refuge following two observation sessions I had had with her infant. This new mother was expressing her lack of confidence in being a mother and wanting access to outside specialist help so she would know she was doing a good job and that her baby was ok. A great deal was going on in the refuge and given the infant's age, many appointments were being made, including with child protection. Numerous intrusions occurred during our session and as these occurred the infant would become increasingly distressed, mirroring what I believed was her mother's distress and anxiety. The mother was, however, able to calm herself, and did so through the act of comforting her baby, and to great effect for the baby as well. I had seen this time and time again in the previous two observations I had with her and her baby, so I shared this observation with this mother as she was doing this with her infant. This was powerful for her. My observation did not minimise what is a normal desire for reassurance for a first-time mother, but offered her something real, tangible and comforting to internalise about herself in her new role as mother.

You can overt the infant or child's behaviours when you see them happen in the presence of the parent, whether they are positive or not. For example, perhaps an infant may flinch or jump when their parent's voice is raised. Talking directly with the infant you may say, 'oh my goodness, did you get frightened then? So did I'; or the toddler who watches every move their parent makes but will not return their gaze when the parent looks at them, 'I've noticed little Darcy is very curious about what you are doing all the time but does not like to let you see this and turns her head when you look at her. What do you think that's about?'; or the child who becomes very still when the subject of the violence at home is being discussed and their parent becomes upset, 'I wonder what it feels like for Sanjay to hear you talk about what has happened at home? What might he tell me if I was to ask him about the things he remembers?' You will be able to ask some children directly in front of their parent about their experience and for others wonder aloud 'what might they tell me about the violence if they could put this into words?'

Infant- and child-led work with parents is about introducing the parent to the idea of their child having their own personality, their own experience and their own point of view. This can occur even when the infant or child is not with you in the room. You can ask such questions as, 'what might Cecily be doing right now if she was here with us talking about her dad?' or 'what might Cecily tell us about what she misses about her dad if she was here now?' Your mind set is to bring the infant or child physically or figuratively into the working space and therapeutic relationship you form with the parent. As was discussed in the first chapters of this book, this work starts with you having the infant or child at the forefront of your mind. What then flows are the possibilities of working in such a way that you bring the subjectivity of every parent's child into their minds through every contact and conversation you have with them. This is a balanced process where neither the infant/child nor parent dominates the reflective space, and the relationship between them becomes an active and alive subject in the space you create.

Present, past and future

Linking the past with the present occurs when you use something that is powerfully and emotionally evocative in the present and connect it with something about the past. For example, when speaking to the new mother in refuge with her newborn you might capture her feelings of inadequacy as you ask a range of potential linking questions. This might be gently asking, 'who was your go-to person when you were very little?', or, 'if you could have anyone in your world with you right now to reassure you, who might that be? What is it about this person who sets them apart from others in your life?' Further to these, and of course, depending on this new mother's answers, you could also explore, 'when you were little, how did you find comfort when you felt distressed?', or, 'what were the things that made you feel like your baby seems to be feeling right now, when you were a little girl?' A future question might be, 'when your little baby becomes a mother herself, who do you imagine she will go to for reassurance?' If she was to answer, 'my daughter will come to me', you may reflect, 'what will you provide to her that perhaps your mother or father did not provide to you?' Perhaps you may wonder aloud, 'what will need to happen for you and your daughter both to remain as connected as you are now, as she gets older and starts to show you when she wants her own way or maybe to try things for herself?'

Possibilities about the future are very powerful for parents to consider, particularly when their own past relationships with their parents have been marred by violence, abuse or neglect. Where the infant or child is not present you can still move back and forward in time. You may ask a parent to tell you what it was like when their infant was born and they first met their child. You many ask the parent what they know of their own birth and how their parents felt about their arrival in the world. Should they not know, you may want to ask them to imagine what their parents may have felt. Moving forward you could ask about what might need to happen between now and the time when their child is older for their child to want them involved in their child's future important life events, for example, the birth of their own child, their child's wedding or regular catch-ups or telephone calls. An extremely powerful area to explore with parents who have perpetrated violence is to wonder about what their relationship will be like with their children when their children are adults. Added to this is the exploration of what they, the parent/s, might need to do to achieve this.

Strategies for difference

The strategies previously mentioned for enhancing reflection and providing experiences that help parents and their children to integrate new ways of thinking and of being together. Some parents find more structured suggestions helpful. These involve such ideas as 'Watch, Wait, Wonder' (Cohen 2006; Cohen *et al.* 1999; Cohen *et al.* 2002) and 'Match, Mismatch and Repair' (Tronick 2007; Tronick & Beeghly 2011) as referred to in Chapter Two. Examples of Ed Tronick's work can be found by looking on the internet. His 'Still Face Experiment' videos are very powerful. Another accessible way for parents to understand their infant/child and the importance of providing them with healthy, safe relationships is provided by 'The Circle of Security' (Hoffman *et al.* 2006; Marvin *et al.* 2002; Powell *et al.* 2013). This intervention model is based on assessing and then promoting positive attachments and uses the mantra 'Bigger. Stronger, Kinder and Wise' to refer to the parent's role in relation to their child. Again, more information about this model is found readily on the internet. Circle of Security uses a very clever metaphor involving what they call 'Shark Music' (from the movie *Jaws*) which plays in the parent's mind and gets in the way of them being emotionally available to their child as their past experiences mislead them into thinking that intimacy with their child involves danger and must be avoided.

I also use the metaphor of 'The Umbrella' to explain how past trauma can interfere with present and future healthy relationships. I explain that when our life experience has taught us that the world is a stormy place, we can learn that it is best to be always ready with our trusty umbrella. If those storms have been often, lashing and frightening we may have learnt that it is better to keep the umbrella up at all times.

We can pass this lesson onto our children, teaching them to expect the world to be stormy place, and not to expect any sun. This can be a useful lesson for our children as sometimes the umbrella keeps them protected. The trouble is that the world is not always stormy. When you have your umbrella open it makes it difficult to see your child properly as the umbrella gets in the way.

If the child has their umbrella also always up, then you both find it difficult to see each other. Holding the umbrellas on those days when it is sunny also makes it hard to play, to hug, to laugh together and to enjoy the good weather. In fact, if you only ever have your umbrella up, when do you know the difference between a stormy day and a sunny, cloudy, windy, frosty, hot, smoggy or cloudless day?

You can then explore what happens when you try to put your umbrella down sometimes, just to see what the weather is like outside? Are there times when the umbrella gets in the way of enjoying the day? What might happen if your child too should also put down their umbrella on those sunny days? What other things might you be able to do or see when the umbrella comes down?

Our ways of protecting ourselves are usually learnt very early and are physiologically stored in our bodies. We should not and cannot simply put our defences (umbrellas) permanently away. How adults and children have learnt to defend themselves from trauma must be respected. Defending yourself when no one else is available, or able to, is what has kept some people, literally and psychologically, alive! Our job as workers is not to strip away a person's defences but to respect them. These defences (or umbrellas) may have served them well at a time when they needed them most. Unfortunately, defences become our default position when we are under, or feel like we are under, attack. This can be real or imagined. If you have been abused or exposed to trauma early and repeatedly in life then your body holds a physiological response to cope with this assault to your physical, emotional and/or relational experience. We feel the world before we think about the world even if the time fraction between feeling to action only takes nano-seconds (Cozolino 2008). Instead of taking away a child or parent's umbrella, we need to focus on expanding their repertoire of responding. The younger someone is the quicker they will develop different and more varied ways of responding. Nevertheless, cognitive strategies such as thinking, 'up goes my umbrella', or, 'I can hear the shark music playing' acts as a circuit breaker and a reminder to think, not simply react.

SUMMARY

The purpose of this chapter is to advocate for the intrinsic value in and importance of healthy play. This is for infants, children and all of us, whatever age or stage in life. Play replenishes and offers creativity in problem solving and managing complex, painful and what can be frightening emotions, memories and experiences. Play eases anxiety, enhances trust and importantly offers relief. Why would an infant, child or adult want to remain in a constant state of pain? Playfulness, in music, singing, games, art and humour can balance out the 'hard bits' that accompany working to address family violence. It is right to make time for play in this work. Our interventions with children, working upwards from a baseline of safety, need to grow with their development and be led by what and how the child makes meaning in their world. Infant- and child-led parent work, ideally, is the perfect complement to enhance the healing that can happen within the adults themselves, and their relationship with their children.

Chapter Seven

We seek closeness to others and none more so than the young child. As the newest member of a family where there is violence, the infant not only possesses the shortest history of trauma but is the quickest to engage in change and to heal. If we can enable ourselves, as well as fathers, mothers, siblings and alternative carers, to engage with the perspective of the infant, we may uncover potentials we never dreamt possible.

Infants and Children as the Entry Points for Change

As discussed in the preceding chapters, infant- or child-led approaches offer previously untapped, or perhaps previously unthought of opportunities, to engage with families who may be difficult to engage and/or to assist:

> Motivation for change in a closed and unyielding system can sometimes emerge from its newest members. As we re-train ourselves to see the world from their eyes and take clear action to affirm and support their views we invite parents to think back to their experience of being parented and how in years to come they want their children to remember them as parents. (Bunston 2008b, p.170)

Currently many of the interventions used with men and women to address family violence involve group work based on psycho-education and 'adult down' approaches. Such approaches tend to target cognitive processes within the adults they intend to help. For this work, expected standards of behaviour and mechanisms of accountability regarding the provision of baseline safety for the infant, child and non-offending parent are non-negotiable (as described in Chapter Three). However, while there is merit in tackling unhelpful thinking or beliefs that guide or reinforce disrespectful behaviours, these may only address what are the surface issues.

Moving beneath the surface to attend to the relational trauma that may drive the belief systems and behaviours we observe is harder to do and more difficult to measure, particularly when trauma begins very early in life and accumulates over time. However, attempting to reach and then heal the source of early, long-standing and complex feelings that underpin problematic behaviours can result in life changes that will be sustained. This work involves going back and reconnecting with the past to re-imagine the present. As workers, we can engage with the pull relationships have in the lives of those we work with, both positive and negative. Relational pulls operate as some of the most powerful motivators in our lives. The most enduring, valued and influential attachments we have are most often with our parents, siblings, partner and children. Destructive responses to the fear of losing an important relationship can be marked by using violence, with the intention of controlling or forcing those relationships to continue, irrespective of how that harms the other person. However, positive responses can also result when a person fears losing the relationships that matter most to them if change does not occur. This might involve the loss of a relationship (through their departure and/or emotional withdrawal) with a child and/or a partner and child, if violence in the home continues. We can exploit the pull of relationships in a way which grows rather than destroys.

Recovery and healing after trauma for adults includes 'the identification of new possibilities for their lives or the possibility of taking a new and different path in life' (Vázquez 2013, p.32). Three broad categories of growth have been suggested by Calhoun & Tedeschi (2014). These involve, 'changes in the perception of self, changes of the experience of relationships with others, changes in one's general philosophy of life' (p.5). Another study undertaken to explore the recovery process for women who had left a violent relationship found that many, through the process of 'rebuilding their lives experienced growth in their self-awareness, faith, and inter-personal relationships' (Anderson et al. 2012, p.1289). How each person impacted by trauma will respond is different following the cessation of the trauma. Our body is designed to cope with stress. When the body no longer feels danger, it generally calms down. However, this depends on how often, and how early we have been exposed to trauma. Work with infants, children or adults who have perhaps experienced a singular trauma, associated with an accident, illness or environmental disaster may find that 'the normal path is recovery, which is facilitated by a supportive environment and relief of distress associated with memories of the event... It is likely that early intervention could facilitate recovery in individuals at risk for development of PTSD' (Yehuda 2004, p.35).

Relational trauma within family relationships is different. The complexities of the ongoing relational pulls involved in family violence make this area of trauma work one of the most difficult to navigate. For infants and children, relational trauma is also not straightforward as children often remain in contact with parents or family who have caused them harm. This contact, if not through residing with the person perpetrating the violence, can occur through court ordered access visits, even if this is not the child's stated preference. Shared custody arrangements may be in place, or where parents separate, reconciliations may occur. Alternatively, and despite the risks, children may still want continued contact with the offending parent. We need to find 'ports of entry' at early stages where parents, infants and children may be most available and most receptive to change (Jordan 2012; Stern 2003).

The birth of a child is a profound life-changing event for the mother, bio-physiologically, emotionally and psychologically, and in my work over many years with children affected by family violence, I have found that mothers tend to be more motivated to seek and make use of help when their child is younger, particularly during the child's infancy. Being the parent of a new infant is also one of the major motivating factors for a parent to leave a violent relationship for the safety and wellbeing of their child (Bunston 2016; Bunston *et al.* 2016; Rasool 2015). Research suggests that women who leave violent relationships soon after the birth have healthier and more secure attachments with their child by age four than women who remain in a violent relationship (Levendosky *et al.* 2011).

The birth of a child may be similarly life changing for a father. The family violence sector has not explored how much might be achieved by engaging with fathers at this time. While the motivation for a father who uses violence to change and accept help remains possible at many different life stages, the birth of a child may provide a pivotal opportunity for some men to reappraise their life, in the same way as it can for women. The new challenges of parenting an infant may possibly overwhelm and trigger existing inadequacies in managing relational stress. Early parenthood is a time of increased vulnerability for all, but it is also a time of increased opportunity. Early in the journey fathers are more likely to be in contact with services, attend pre- and post-natal appointments and be present at the birth and during the hospital admission.

Family violence work tends to happen after violence occurs, not before. Work with men generally, and fathers specifically, has tended to occur because of court ordered sanctions, police involvement or because a partner threatens to, or does, leave with the children. The potential loss of a relationship with their child may spur a father on to make considerable efforts to accept help to change. 'It is vital to support fathers who wish to eliminate their violent behaviour and become positively engaged in their children's lives' (Labarre *et al.* 2016, p.3). We have much to learn through safely and creatively discovering different and more proactive ways to engage with fathers and mothers who use violence or are the victims of violence in their most intimate relationships.

This chapter looks at four different ways to intervene to address the impact on infants and children of family violence. Each of these ways includes targeting family violence during periods when families and/or individuals are most receptive to change during the parenting stages involved with their infant and young children. This also includes where infants and children are removed from one or both parents. These settings include:

- group work

- family work

- refuge-based work

- foster care work.

WORKING WITH MOTHERS, FATHERS AND INFANTS AND YOUNG CHILDREN IN GROUPS

Group work interventions are commonly used in addressing family violence. This approach does not suit everyone or every situation. However, the strength in group work sits with the opportunity to use the rich interactional material, group dynamics and relational politics that arise in groups to facilitate healing (Bunston, Pavlidis & Leyden 2003). When the myriad of relational processes that occur within a group are managed thoughtfully and skilfully, change can be accelerated beyond what is often possible in individual work. Furthermore, the reverberations of relational traumas from the past can be captured in the present and unpacked in such a way as to facilitate healing for the whole group (Bunston, Pavlidis & Cartwright 2016). This is often achieved through attending to the ebb and flow of the group and following the group dynamic, over and above the content planned for the group. Having some plan for what you will do is useful to follow, but only in so far as it allows you to use what arises in the group. The nature of groups often leads to relational material being available in the here-and-now of the group relationships which invokes relational anxieties or relational challenges as the group members form connections with one another. As these relational dramas, exchanges and stories arise they can be reworked, reflected on and reconsidered both cognitively and emotionally with empathy and respect (Bunston 2017).

When we keep group members feeling safe enough, we have a chance to visit painful, shameful and traumatic memories. It is essential that such deep work, as well as developing the capacity to both identify and then learn how to use these moments, is supported through accessing good, regular supervision (Bunston 2013a). This approach to group work should not be undertaken by one facilitator alone. The group facilitators must then be supported in this complex and highly evocative area of work and have their own supported space to reflect. Supervision is one space (and is discussed in more depth in Chapter Eight). Facilitators writing up process notes together, the creation of a therapeutic newsletter (see Appendix Four), reading research and practice articles or attending training, all promote reflection and integration of learning in our practice. Most importantly, group work is most effective for us, and the parents, when their infants and young children are central to the group space and offer the reason for the group to come together in the first place (see Appendix Three for more information on infants and mother, infants and father, and children and parent groups).

Case example: Franklin (8 months) and Mary (28)

Mary was a participant in a group for infants and their mothers who had experienced family violence. Mary did not have custody of her infant. Franklin remained in the care of his father, Paul, as he had been assessed by child protection as the more protective parent. The court made an order for Mary to attend the group but as we were not a court mandated or funded program, we did not accept Mary's referral into the group until we met Mary and Franklin together and assessed whether or not Franklin felt safe enough in his mother's company to attend. Child protection did not attend the pre-group assessment session. We met with Mary and let her know that this group was for her and Franklin and we would not report back to child protection unless both Mary, and if appropriate Franklin, were present and involved in the feedback. This aligned us with Mary. However, we made it clear to Mary that if we felt the group experience was adversely affecting Franklin, we would not have him continue in the group.

Mary was often loud and crass, but she was also likeable and keen to build a relationship with Franklin. Mary acknowledged to the group that there had been reciprocal violence in her relationship with Franklin's father Paul, but that the main reason for the court not awarding her care of her son was due to substance abuse that she stated she was now managing appropriately. Franklin was both curious about his mother and apprehensive in his response to her. He tended to go to the group facilitators before his mother. He would circle around her, but not approach. Mary often became very agitated when speaking about Paul and at these times Franklin would move to the other side of the room. When we brought this to Mary's attention, she would check herself briefly but would soon return to criticising Paul. On one occasion Mary began swearing and became very loud. I called out 'stop' in a loud voice, and she did. She looked at me, stunned, as did the rest of the group. The group fell silent. I then said, 'You are scaring Franklin with your loud voice and you are scaring me as well.' I immediately felt guilty and went on to say that I did not mean to frighten her or the group but explained why I felt I needed to call her to account. I asked her not to swear again and not to frighten Franklin or other group members. I explained I understood why she felt so upset towards at her ex-partner and losing custody of her son.

In our facilitators' group supervision, immediately after the group, I spoke about this incident and my worry that I had simply mirrored what Mary had done. I felt ashamed that I had not handled this better and thought that Mary might not now return to the group. Our supervisor was very reassuring. As I unpacked the event, we explored how what I had done may have matched what Mary did in its intensity, but not in its intent, manner or aftermath. We explored my growing attachment to Mary and Franklin, despite Mary's abrasive language and manner. To my great relief, Mary and Franklin returned to group the following week. The tone of the group shifted and Mary began to self-monitor her behaviour and asked for more input on how to make Franklin feel safe. The impact this had on the whole group was very powerful. The group began to feel more settled and safe. We revisited the previous week's incident and how everyone felt this week. I spoke about my fear of losing Mary and Franklin and how I did not want this to happen. The other mothers where open to discussing ways they might either frighten, ignore or push their infants away. They also talked about events that had frightened them in their own childhoods and who it was that frightened them. This conversation had a profound effect on the group. The infants themselves gave their mothers, the other mothers, and the other infants, direct behavioural and emotional feedback about what made them feel safe, happy, sad, confused or distressed, which we could all observe, reflect on and then respond to.

This incident demonstrates the capacity for repair and restoration which can occur in a group setting. Through the relational steps taken with Mary at the very beginning of the group she felt as though she had been welcomed into the group as a mother with her son Franklin, not because the court had ordered this but because she had been through an assessment like every other group member coming to the group. In this group, Mary felt that she had been given a chance. My 'stop' was loud but not abusive. Congruently, I spoke to what I saw Franklin feeling and what I felt. I felt affirmed by the supervision session and could sit with my apprehension and anxiety about losing this infant and mother. Franklin began to feel protected by the group and by the end of the group was not only approaching his mother but had begun to sit on her lap. This positive affirmation provided by Franklin to his mother was more powerful than anything that could have been spoken. The ripple from the event provided a space for open and healthy discussion in the group about how each one of us can impact the infants through our unthinking behaviours. It also opened a window to the past which helped make sense of things that had frightened them and how they might protect their infants from this happening again for them.

As I and my colleagues became more skilled and experienced in running these groups we became more confident about how we would approach talking about uncomfortable topics, conflicts or awkward moments. When toddlers went to others over their parent for comfort, or infants would look away from their parent or constantly go to sleep, we would gently wonder what this might be telling us, and telling their parent. The child who would stiffen at their parent's touch or be mesmerised by the sound of their voice when singing would be noticed and wondered about. The child who desperately pulls himself away from his parent is saying something very clearly and loudly, yet we often fear putting this into words for the child or helping them, with us, to make sense of this for them and for their parent. The capacity to talk about painful feelings in the group setting, as they happen, is very delicate and very powerful work. All the parents in that particular group had, at some time or another felt unwanted by, inadequate with, or hostile towards their child. We can make tolerable what are often intolerable thoughts and feelings felt by the parents and expressed by the child.

Therapeutic group work with infants and toddlers is different to group work for older children. The infant and toddler's world is their caregiver, and as such, developmentally, the work for infants and caregivers needs to have them together. Older children often benefit from group opportunities away from their caregiver, but work best when their carer is also involved actively in the therapeutic process (see Appendix Three). Fathers, whether they are present in their infant/children's lives or not, and whether we like it or not, are also crucial. We must find ways to engage and involve them early in the work. In my years of working with children and mothers, the fathers are like ghosts in the group room and their presence keenly felt (Bunston 2001, 2006, 2008a, 2008b). Rather than idealise or demonise them, it is important to hold onto what is good enough of the father for the sake of their infant. As the product of both parents, the infant needs something good to take from both, helping them to grow their sense of identity as connected to, but also separate from, both their mother and father (Jones & Bunston 2012). Exploring how the mothers can hold something good of the infant or child's father despite his violent or controlling behaviours is also important in making clear their infant was not 'just like their father' and was emerging into being 'just like themselves'.

My work with infants and older children has shown me that most of them love their dads and many remain in contact with him. There is still much work to be done in this arena and their remains a dearth of fathering programs within the family violence sector (Labarre *et al.* 2016). Opportunities to work safely with infants, children and their fathers are possible. My colleagues and I developed one such group work intervention for infants, toddlers, young children and their fathers (Bunston 2013b). This work, as with the older children's groups, targeted men who had successfully been through a men's behaviour change program. The group work intervention was modelled on the infant/mother groups we had previously developed and we focused on helping the fathers to experience play and to read their children's relational cues and appreciate their child's subjectivity. The group also explored how these fathers could keep their children safe emotionally and physically, and to see first-hand how their behaviour impacts directly on their child's experience of themselves and their emerging little personalities (Bunston 2013b). The case example of Ajay (4) and Joss (6) in Chapter Six illustrates how Ajay's emotional expression was being impacted by his father's dismissal of his distress, robbing them of any intimacy as a father and son. In Chapter Five we saw Stephanie (12 weeks) teach Tom (27) in a very powerful way just how much his fighting with her mother impacted on her sense of wellbeing and safety. Susie (4), Joshie (5) and Arnold (29) in Chapter Six demonstrated beautifully the reciprocity of play and how this developed when pleasurable engagement became possible for these children and their father within the safety of the group.

FAMILY WORK

Family work is not often recommended or possible when there is severe and ongoing violence. Nor is it appropriate to allow an infant or child remain in an environment where neither parent can adequately protect or cannot demonstrate a commitment to protecting their child/ren. There will be instances where child protection has assessed that a family can remain together if certain conditions are adhered to. As stated above, there may also be windows of opportunity to engage with families before the violence increases in severity and frequency. While challenges remain, some Aboriginal communities within Australia have set up community initiated and led programs that work towards cultural healing for families and communities impacted by family violence (Neave, Faulkner & Nicholson 2016; Ombudsman 2015). This work recognises that the violence experienced in their communities is predominantly by men towards women and children. However, it also speaks of a need to be inclusive of men and to invite them to participate in finding solutions (IFVPF 2008).

Involving men in solutions for addressing family violence or family conflicts, where it is safe to do so, has been recognised as integral to the cessation of violence and subsequent opportunities for familial healing. This applies when couples choose to stay together, and when they do not (Fletcher & StGeorge 2010; Goldner *et al.* 1990). Within prisons, interventions for serious offenders of violence and sexual assault also see the need to draw on men's primary desire for forming relationships. For example, an intervention model for serious offenders developed in New Zealand, looks at tapping into the strengths and motivations of offenders by developing and reflecting on the relationships created within a therapeutic community. The 'Good Lives Model' is strengths-based and includes, amongst other capacities identified, the use of relatedness, play, spirituality and pleasure in their intervention. This model commits to 'viewing offenders as fellow human beings with similar needs and life aspirations' and reminds us that 'like all humans, offenders strive to achieve certain primary human goods in their lives' (Fortune, Ward & Polaschek 2014, p.98). These 'human goods' refer to personal and relational achievements and wishes.

We need to balance what is desired, and what is achievable. Family work is different to group work in intensity and in risk. While group culture and membership can be used very successfully to motivate individual adult group members to work on managing their emotional responses appropriately, family work often deals with old patterns. Fault lines can arise very quickly, and can be more volatile where peer pressure is not present to keep individuals in check. Within group work interventions the desire to be accepted or approved of by the group is a very organising principle. We often see individuals adjust their behaviour accordingly. In family work, good behaviour may be present for a time but then poorly developed interpersonal and/or conflict management skills lead to reoccurring conflicts and power imbalances.

Case example: Jason (7), Anna (12), Sandra (35) and Phillip (37)

Jason had been re-referred to the child and adolescent mental health service where I was working. He was suffering from acute anxiety and he had begun to refuse to attend school. Jason had difficulties going to sleep, he suffered from nightmares and he often reported feeling sick. His doctor found little evidence of any physical basis for Jason's ill-health. Jason, now seven, had been first seen by the mental health service for bed-wetting and soiling when he was five. These difficulties coincided with an acrimonious separation by his parents. Both his mother and father acknowledged they were verbally abusive towards the other. Jason and his sister Anna had regular access to their father and reported feeling safe and enjoying their time when staying with him. Phillip had recently begun a relationship with a woman who had two children of her own. All the children reportedly got on well and enjoyed each other's company.

Over a couple of months, I saw Jason alone, with his sister, and with his mother and sister. Jason spoke a great deal about his father. When I broached the possibility of involving Phillip in some sessions to discuss shared parenting issues, Sandra reluctantly agreed. Based on the reports of the previous worker who had seen this family, I was not convinced that Sandra and Phillip would be able to keep the emotional safety of their children utmost in their minds when meeting as a family unit. I arranged to meet first with this separated couple together, and not with the children. The session soon deteriorated as I asked both how they managed working together to parent their children now they were no longer a couple. Sandra began to berate Phillip for not spending time alone with his children now he had his new family. Phillip got up and pulled a chair over as he stormed out of the room.

I sat and waited in silence with Sandra until Phillip returned some ten minutes later, having gone outside for a cigarette. I remained sitting in silence for a little longer as I watched both parents become increasingly uncomfortable. I gently then commented on what it might feel like to be Jason and Anna when their dad and mum behaved in the same way I had just experienced. I told Phillip how I felt quite afraid when he pushed over the chair and now wondered whether it was safe enough for us to continue meeting. As both began to launch into attack mode about the behaviour of the other, I stood up and stated that I was wrong to ask them to sit together to try to help them think together about how we might help their son. I apologised for putting them in such a difficult position. Both settled very quickly and asked if we could try again. Phillip expressed that he did want to be involved in supporting both his children. For the remainder of the session we worked out the rules for how this session would proceed, and what baseline needed to be met for Jason and Anna to feel safe, and how we might devise a plan where all the family was involved in supporting Jason. I also informed both parents that my primary objective was to keep Jason feeling safe and said I would not organise any future meetings unless Jason gave me his seal of approval to do so.

We never did meet as the original family unit. I asked Jason to assess how we could best involve family members based on when and with whom he felt most safe and in what situations. My work involved helping Jason work out what made him feel safe and how I could support his family, who did love him, to know what to do to best assist him. I met with Sandra and Phillip on another two occasions to review how they felt Jason was progressing, and did so with Jason's knowledge. The family members met in different configurations over several months and the family worked hard to find new ways to develop 'good enough' conflict management strategies to allow Jason to get on with being a child rather than him feeling consumed by the conflict between his warring parents.

At the commencement of this family work it was hard to know if any benefit would come from endeavouring to engage with the whole family. However, Jason was in regular contact with his father, wanted him involved and expressed greater ambivalence about his relationship with his mother than with his father. The abusive relationship between these two parents seemed to hit Jason harder than his sister. Perhaps this was because their relationship had worsened by the time Jason arrived. Perhaps his temperament was less robust than his sister's. Research suggests that boys have slower developmental growth than girls and are impacted differently by exposure to early relational trauma. 'This difference shows up, perhaps most notably, in small boys' behaviour; they are less able to self-regulate and more in need of emotional and regulatory support from caregivers (Golding & Fitzgerald 2016, p.13). The difficulties for Jason appeared to lay in his parents' inability, even while not living together, to productively co-parent their son. Whether I met with his father or not, Jason loved his dad and was having regular contact with him. If I could undertake family work to facilitate enough of a shift in the way his parents parented, then I was alleviating some of the relational stress which was so damaging to Jason's healthy development.

The level of conflict between this couple may not be considered as severe as occurs within other families; however, the ongoing, persistent disharmony and emotionally abusive conflict between Sandra and Phillip was debilitating for Jason. What these parents had in common was their love for their son, not for each other. I have found a shared commitment to children an extremely powerful motivator with other parents I have worked with when undertaking family work (Bunston 2008b, 2015). I made an assessment that Jason was physically safe but not emotionally safe. Had the level of conflict continued I would have made a notification to child protection. This was something I spoke to his parents about in our first joint session. Jason was my barometer. I had no idea other than what he and his family told me about their progress. But Jason did return to school, his nightmares lessened, as did his ill-health. Jason was not responsible for ensuring his parents behaved. Their attachment to him was responsible for their motivation to make changes they had not previously been able to consider.

WORKING IN REFUGES

The purpose of women's refuges is to provide women and children exposed to family violence with somewhere safe to live. Sometimes the number of children in refuge outstrip the number of women, yet there are few, and sometimes no, specific workers allocated to children (Bunston 2016). Of the children in refuge, those aged four and below make up the highest numbers (AIHW 2012a, 2012b; Shinn 2010). However, it would be rare to find a refuge which employed an infant- or toddler-specific worker. The role of the children's workers is often underfunded, and on occasion, undervalued (Bunston 2016). The infant or young child is least likely to receive any direct or even indirect attention from refuge staff, despite being the main reason behind their mother's decision to access refuge (Bunston 2016). This means that the infant and/or child/mother relationship is least likely to be worked with directly by staff, despite being potentially the most powerful entry point for accelerating relational healing.

The previous chapter provided the case example of Anika (2), Terry (4½) and Shirley (31) who were in their second week of refuge. Through engaging the two children and mother together in play, an important piece of work became possible. When infants, children and mothers first enter refuge, much time can be spent doing paperwork, making appointments, talking through rules, sorting out meals, bedding, clothes and the provision of all sorts of material aid. While practical needs are important, infants and children would be better served by having their emotional needs attended to. When the mother is unable to do this herself, then others need to step in to assist infants and children to manage the distress of entering a new and strange place, and to manage the feelings about the events which led them to fleeing home and the anxiety they may feel about who and what they have left behind (Bunston & Sketchley 2012). Ideally, this emotional support should be offered to the mother as well as her child/ren, as a family unit. Simply being 'truly with' families who are generally highly traumatised and significantly distressed is, in the long term, much more important than 'the doing of things for or to' them in order to address their immediate material wellbeing. The desire to put the 'office work' ahead of the 'relational work' can sometimes reflect a worker's anxiety, and the promotion of bureaucratic tasks in refuge can be a way to avoid the pain of attending to the distress of the infant, child or mother (Bunston 2016).

Refuges are unique settings offering amazing opportunities to provide early intervention to children and mothers who have experienced and are clearly most at risk of family violence. As has been well documented, women are likely to return to violent relationships (Gondolf 1988; Walker 1979). Tapping into what will engage and grow the relational bond between mother and infant/ child is potentially the most important work that a refuge can offer (Bunston 2011). Benefit can be gained by staff making time simply to sit with infants, children and mothers. The families who enter refuge sometimes struggle with knowing how to be with one another. They may know little other than how to operate in survival mode. Sitting and playing together, talking together and/or eating together may not have been experienced or even possible. In refuge, they are given a new opportunity to express themselves free from the fear of violence. Leaving the violence does not automatically ensure recovery, or new ways of relating to one another. This happens through experiencing and being supported in developing different relational opportunities. Those in the best position to offer relational experiences of difference are the refuge staff. They do this by simply being with the women and the children who seek refuge with them.

Case example: Mel (4) and Tessa (6)

For my PhD thesis, I undertook research within a range of different refuges. Some were in other parts of Australia and some were overseas. I had a limited time of only one week to visit a particular refuge; I was hoping that during that time a mother and infant (12 months or under) might arrive at the refuge and be prepared to participate in my study. I spent my first two days simply 'hanging out' at this refuge. There was a grandmother, Naomi, with her granddaughter, Tessa, aged 6, and a mother, Marna, with her daughter, Mel, aged 4, currently staying at the refuge. Staff informed me that it was unlikely that Marna would talk to me as she found it difficult to trust newcomers, however, they gave me permission to meet with residents should they choose to talk to me. I was introduced to some of the women in the kitchen/lounge area and I sat on a kitchen stool next to Naomi while she made a late breakfast for herself and Tessa. As I was chatting to Naomi and Tessa I noticed a little girl. This little girl slowly emerged from the bedrooms and shyly slipped outside to the play area just off from the lounge. Mel was intrigued by Tessa. Whenever I looked her way she would avert her eyes and busy herself with the toy basket. Tessa finished breakfast and went outside to join Mel. Tessa started a ball game but quickly became impatient as Mel had trouble catching the ball. I asked if I could join in. Tessa was quick to agree and Mel shyly nodded her agreement.

I spent the next two hours playing with these two little girls. Ball games, toy stories, and hide and seek, where I was mostly the seeker and not often granted a chance to hide. I was exhausted but exhilarated. Mel's mother seemed particularly amused by me and said she had never seen a worker play like this before. I sat down next to her and explained who I was and why I was there. She did not want to be involved in my research, but agreed to sit and chat with me about her experiences over years of contact with refuges. Afterwards I settled down with Naomi and played cards. I learnt an enormous amount about these two girls and their carers. Tessa and her grandmother left the refuge later that day but the next morning Mel allowed me to play the ball game again with her. During our thirty minutes of play, I noticed how significantly her hand-eye co-ordination improved as did her ease in talking to me.

I recognise that as a trained therapist my job is to know how to talk to people. I also acknowledge that I had the time to play with these two girls and to sit and chat with their carers. I have spent a considerable amount of time delivering programs, visiting and researching within refuges. I have consistently had workers tell me that I have been able to find out more about the women and children residing in their refuges in one session than they, as workers, have been able to discover in weeks or sometimes even months. I do not report this back to boast. The difference, I believe, is that I am not impeded by a culture and work practices and protocols that tend to foster reactivity over reflectiveness. My intention was to play, talk and discover. If refuges were supported and funded to 'slow down' and to focus on providing emotional refuge as well as physical refuge, the results in healing and change might become both more rapid and more lasting (Glennen 2011). Where the persistent focus is on the mother as the entry point for change, and where the mother is seen as the one responsible for providing the refuge for their infant, even when they are in no state to do so, we will limit opportunities for healing. Conversely:

> the sooner the infant is responded to and their subjectivity and inter-subjectivity acknowledged, the sooner will there come opportunities to capitalise on the relational hope the mother carries for her infant and herself. These mothers largely accessed Refuge in order to create a different future. Refuge is in a unique position to start at the very beginning with these infants and mothers in working towards the realisation of this goal. (Bunston 2016, pp.247–248)

This way of working need not cost significantly more money, but it will call for a greater investment in time to grow infant- and child-led relational recovery (Bunston & Glennen 2015). The investment mothers make in leaving violent relationships to give their children refuge can be exploited constructively. This is a unique opportunity when the mother has taken a huge step to improve her infant and/or child's, as well as her own, future.

When the mother and child arrive together to refuge they both need healing. We cannot keep asking the wounded mother to heal the wounded child. We need attentive, relationally available and nurturing others who take time to be there emotionally and to actively support the child/mother relationship in their journey through refuge. We can accelerate what Humphreys, Thiara & Skamballis (2011) call the mother and child's relational 'readiness for change'. By attending to the cues of the infants and children together with the mother, we can help restore what enlivens them rather than what depletes them.

FOSTER CARE

Foster carers act as contingent caregivers. They are the back-up caregiver, either through the provision of respite when needed or for temporary periods of time after which the child goes on to another placement or returns to the care of their parent or extended family. In instances where they become the permanent carers, they are 'the acting parent', but of course they will never be the biological parent. This means they step into the role of parent but the circumstances of why the child is in care and the potency of the link to their biological parent always lingers, both for the child and the foster carers. At some level the child is aware that some rupture or loss has occurred around their relationship with their parent. The foster carer, while able to love and show love to the child, may also have ideas about what this child should be like. They may have their limits tested more readily than if this was their own biological child. It has been suggested that infants and young children in foster care have three critical needs that should be met by their carers. These are that their behavioural cues are understood properly, that they are nurtured, and that the 'caregivers provide children with a predictable inter-personal environment such that children develop better regulatory capabilities' (Dozier *et al.* 2002, p.541).

Infants and children who enter foster care do so because their parents are unable to care for them. Generally, despite having been removed from a home where there has been significant violence, the residue of trauma remains. The infant and child will know they are in a different environment and may continue to use the same behaviours to protect themselves from possible and/or anticipated stress or trauma. They cannot usually verbalise what they may have been through. They communicate through their behaviours and relational responses, which inform us about their experience. These behaviours can be jarring, disturbing and, at times, repelling. It may be hard to like or nurture these children because their defence mechanisms are so rigid and unyeilding that attempts to get past them can leave the foster carer feeling inadequate, unwanted and unappreciated. It takes time for such engrained behaviours to develop in one so very young. It will take time, and calm, thoughtful and consistently nurturing caregiving, for these little ones to come out of their shells. This is in part because they experience a loss of what is familiar, even if that familiar has been violent.

Foster carers, like refuge workers, do not undertake this role for the money. Some might say that they end up paying for the privilege of being a foster carer. Paradoxically, these caregiving roles can give so much value to those they care for, yet the foster and refuge caregiving role is often not adequately valued in society generally. Foster carers do an important and undervalued job, but they are human and inevitably bring their own feelings and experiences with them. The motivation to fulfil such roles can be worth reflecting on. There is nothing wrong with meeting some of our own needs through a caring role, unless it precludes our ability to recognise just why we want certain needs met and how we can also find other ways to fulfil ourselves, other than simply through our work. The reflective foster carer, refuge worker and family violence worker may benefit from asking the question, 'what do I get out of this role?'

It is the intensity of the caregiving role in foster care, however, that is so profoundly different to other adult involvement with children who are not one's own. The foster child/ren are in your home space. They live with your family. Your role as guardians is monitored by outside professionals who you may feel on occasions demand much and give little. Your capacities as a caregiver can often be tested by the challenging behaviours of the child in your care. The level of distress you see in some children may make you feel hopeless, or highlight that you need more support from the professionals. At times, the cost to you and your family in caring for this child may be too great and you feel compelled to relinquish the care of this child. These are all legitimate and real pressures that are experienced by foster carers at some time or another. Sometimes placements don't work for the family or child, and moving the child can be for the best.

However, it is often within these difficult times of strain that the ability to weather the storm and reflect on what are the most distressing aspects of the foster caregiving relationship reveals something of what this child is asking of you. What then might be involved in meeting this child's needs and how might we find ways of making this relationship worthwhile and reparative for this child?

Case example: Molly (3), Monica (49) and Jerry (45)

Molly came to live with Monica and Jerry after she had been removed from her parents' care because of ongoing family violence. There was a lack of commitment and neither parent demonstrated capacity to protect Molly from harm. Both parents struggled with mental illness and substance abuse. Monica and Jerry had been foster carers for six months. They had grown-up children who had moved out of home and were the grandparents of two small children. They chose to be foster carers at this point in their lives as they had an established business and comfortable family life with more time on their hands. They wanted to 'give back' to the community they lived in. Monica and Jerry described their first weeks with Molly as a dream. She was a sweet and compliant girl. Despite a significant language delay, Molly seemed able to clearly let them know what she wanted.

Three weeks after Molly came to live with them, the foster carers' four-year-old granddaughter, Carly, came to stay for a long weekend while her parents celebrated their wedding anniversary. The two girls appeared to play well together until Carly got on her tricycle, the one she used when she came to visit Nan and Pop. Molly pushed Carly off the tricycle. Carly hit her head and the resulting wound needed stitches. Throughout the incident Molly appeared to show no remorse, nor any concern for Carly. Molly behaved as though everything was normal, despite the swirl of anxiety surrounding the event. Following this incident, Monica and Jerry noticed more of what they described as Molly's almost 'robotic' emotional expression. They became too nervous to leave her and their other grandchildren together in any unsupervised play. Two months after the tricycle incident the family brought home a puppy to replace the family dog which had passed away before Molly came to the family. They found Molly with the puppy under her pillow and were convinced she would have smothered the dog if had they not entered her bedroom in time.

The next day Monica and Jerry made an urgent appointment with their foster care agency. While the family had fortnightly contact with the agency, they felt they needed to discuss the possible ending of Molly's placement. The agency was about to trial a new mentoring program with some of the longer-term and permanent foster carers providing support to new foster carers. This program also offered foster carers an opportunity to book a supervision or debriefing session with one of the senior counsellors from a counselling team which worked within the agency. Monica and Jerry booked in for both the mentoring program and for a debriefing session with the senior counsellor. They also asked for some more intensive support from the agency over the next month while they reviewed their placement with Molly.

The immediate relief of not having to abandon Molly while getting increased support to manage their anxiety about Molly's disconcerting behaviours alleviated some of their fears. Molly's case manager set up twice-weekly home visits over a number of months and spent time talking directly with Molly, and with Monica and Jerry about everyday things, like their new puppy, Sam. As Molly played with Sam the case manager began to talk to Molly about what things Molly thought Sam liked and didn't like, and asked her how did she know? If Sam yelped when Molly tugged at him, the case manager would ask Molly what she thought that meant and what he might feel like. In their debriefing sessions, Monica and Jerry were encouraged to ask Molly more questions about what she felt about different things and to help her explore her choices over which games and books she liked and what games she wanted to play. Monica and Jerry also spent more time explaining their feelings. When they got short tempered or impatient, they would slow themselves down and reassure Molly that everything was ok and even when cranky they would never do anything to hurt her. They remained vigilant when their grandchildren came to play and set up some clear rules with all the children about turn taking and how they were to come to them for help if there were any disputes.

Molly appeared to be a little girl who had a very poor sense of herself. She was developmentally and emotionally delayed and did not seem able to coherently manage her own emotional states nor to recognise feelings in others. Molly's disturbing behaviour in her new home was so 'out of context' it was hard to remain sensitive to the trauma this little girl had endured. Her behaviour was a consequence of trauma. The behaviour heightened the anxiety of her caregivers, and reduced their ability to reflect on what lay behind Molly's 'robotic' behaviour and how they might help. This, naturally enough, raised their concern as they considered the cost to their family in keeping Molly in their care. Fortunately, an effective support system for the foster carers was quickly marshalled which helped contain their anxieties and encouraged them to continue giving Molly something she had not previously experienced. This family offered Molly the opportunity to be in a relationship with carers who could see behind her disconnected emotional self to help her heal. Her foster carers could spend time being with her and talking with her, and together with Molly began to discover who she was when she no longer had to keep herself safe through her compliance or detachment. They could help her develop different ways to both feel and then express what she felt inside and gave her permission to let her guard down.

SUMMARY

We can provide multiple ways to intervene with and support children and their caregiving environment as they heal the devastating sequelae (chronic impacts) of relational violence. There is no 'one size fits all' approach in this area of work. As workers or adults involved in the lives of infants and children impacted by family violence it is our job to be creative, innovative and flexible. The bottom line (or baseline) of safety cannot be compromised, as infants and children must not be left with the responsibility of keeping themselves safe. In 'real-life' this is happening in families where the violence remains secret or has been minimised by services, family members, neighbours and friends. Whole family, infant- and child-led approaches may sometimes be the most appropriate and effective way to intervene to effect change. On other occasions, the removal of the child into foster care or other alternative placements may be the only option. What we need to challenge is the onus often placed on providing adult-focused support in the hope that change will eventually trickle down to the infant and child. Together we must challenge the belief that these youngest, most vulnerable and rapidly developing little ones can afford to wait. They cannot.

Chapter Eight

When I was little I saw the world as such a big place, and dreamt of just how much I would do when I grew up. Now I am big, I see just how little the world is, and my place within it. If I could hold on to the passion, imagination and wonder that I held as a child I could conquer the world...as long as my knees don't give out, and I can have a regular afternoon nap.

Beginning at the Beginning in Our Approach to Addressing Family Violence

I am passionate in my belief that all infants and children deserve to be kept safe, and to feel valued. I know this does not always happen, and as is the human condition, we may never sadly, achieve such an outcome. But we should never give up and we can always strive to do better. This book is written from the perspective of someone who has worked in direct practice with children, infants, and their families, over many years. I have worked largely with highly vulnerable clients, where their voices have not often been considered or included in the debate about, or research relating to, family violence in any comprehensive way.

There is little direct research or evidence I can provide to support my view that what I am advocating for in this book will radically change or prevent the spiralling levels of family violence present within most communities. However, there is also no evidence to suggest that it will not make an important contribution to positive change. Often research papers, presentations and books finish by lamenting the lack of research into their areas of practice. I am not about to say in this last chapter that: 'more research is needed. This statement is so commonplace that the platitude is often ridiculed, particularly by practitioners and policy makers who want clear guidance now, not more muddy studies in a few years' (Emery *et al.* 2016, pp.144–145).

I am saying far more than this. The lack of evidence, or interest in developing and evaluating interventions directly involving infants and young children is largely, from my perspective, because the voice of adults, and the rights of men and women and parents generally, supersedes the rights of infants and young children, and prevents their voices from being heard or comprehensively acted on. There are inadequate levels of funding committed to finding out about and providing services to infants and very young children impacted by family violence. We appear to lack the courage to fully involve, and the commitment to fully invest in, our youngest members in society.

The intention of this book is to focus on what can be done, rather than what cannot. I have retained my passion for this work over many years because I have seen startling and positive changes in infants and young children when they are given a chance. My imagination soars when I think of what is possible should we put our minds to the task of working from the bottom up. Infants and young children have so much to teach us if we will only listen!

This chapter speaks to what we need to put in place at the beginning to aid us in undertaking this healing work successfully. The focus is on three areas:

- the importance of reflective supervision

- re-thinking the 'gender lens' that dominates family violence practice in Western countries

- how to begin at the beginning, in working to address and bring healing from the ravages of family violence.

GROWING 'UP' IN OUR WORK (REFLECTIVE *SUPER*-VISION)

As the preceding chapters have argued, to do this work effectively and appropriately, we need to provide relational support. We ourselves also need to receive relational support. Within my profession as a social worker and family therapist, apart from ongoing learning through study and training, this is done through supervision. This word supervision, and its meaning, is vexed. For some, supervision translates to surveillance or scrutiny. Administrative supervision involves a manager checking on an employee's workload, work performance or work plan. Notice how I use the word 'work' a lot here. Reflective supervision does not serve an administrative function, apart from providing a space for reflective 'good practice'. The type of supervision I am referring to involves a relational exchange, where the supervisor provides a space which feels distinctly different. Certainly an immense amount of work is involved, but it is mostly introspective. If successful, it is also generative. I supervise many workers who are involved in group, family and individual work with infants, children and parents impacted by family violence. I know many workers feel depleted, overwhelmed, frightened or battered because of their work. Infants have died, children have been hospitalised and parents have made threats. One refuge I visited had been fire-bombed by a violent partner. I am aware of some horrific tragedies that have occurred in some refuges and agencies. Such tragedies are not common but they can and do occur and we need to hold this in mind as supervisors and supervisees.

Reflective supervision, if it is provided by someone skilled, experienced and knowledgeable about infant and early childhood and family mental health in the context of family violence, will attend to the baseline emotional and physical safety of the worker. Our work approach needs to mirror our relational approach. Our best chance of building safe therapeutic and healing relationships occurs when we feel safe. Reflective supervision creates a safe, regular, uninterrupted, respected space and reflective process where your work can be explored, your emotional responses unpacked, and the smallest details combed through for meaning. As such:

> Supervision is one of the foundations for compassionate, thoughtful and effective practice. It is essential if we are to grapple with the prejudices and blind spots we all have. Supervision is also necessary to help us think about what we at times would rather not think about – the times when the infant's emotional life is in peril or when the parents are not capable of offering a good enough experience for their infant. (Stone 2016, p.19)

In group, individual, family work and any other therapeutic or caregiving role in relation to infants and children, support is needed to hold the enormity of the feelings aroused by the knowledge of how much they may have suffered, or are still suffering. Staying in touch with our emotional, right brain selves, and remaining reflective enough to integrate what we feel with the meanings that resonate within this work, as well as how this influences what and how we do what we do, is imperative. Reflective supervision makes the commitment to a space to feel, and to think about what we feel (Bunston 2013a). This is something the infants, children and families we work with cannot often afford to do, as reflection can only occur when we feel safe, and not on high alert, or at the ready to defend ourselves. Additionally, this reflective space needs to offer a space to think protectively, not just about the emotional, but also the physical safety of workers and the families we work with.

While procedures should be in place in most organisations regarding worker safety, in creatively working with children, simple safety procedures can sometimes be overlooked. I have provided supervision to group facilitators where the group being run for the children was run in a stand-alone, child-friendly building. The workers had not considered a safety plan for themselves, or the children, should an offending, non-custodial parent suddenly appear. In other instances, workers have been expected to take high numbers of extremely difficult family violence cases either individually and/or within therapeutic groups. This was because their direct role was with infants and children and their workplace considered this work to be not as demanding as the work of their colleagues who worked with adults. When home visits are involved, processes need to be developed to assess whether it is safe to visit someone's home. Similarly, practices need to be thought about regarding how you ensure you remain safe once in someone's home. We cannot always plan for all contingencies in this complex area of practice. But we can create pause for thought, and take steps to think through safe practices which ensure our emotional, psychological and physical wellbeing.

WHEN A 'GENDER ONLY' LENS FAILS INFANTS AND CHILDREN

This book places the infant and child front and centre in our work. There are very real and very important reasons for considering family violence from a gendered perspective. There are significantly higher rates of men who use physical violence than women, and who have greater access to resources and power in our society, and who abuse these privileges across all strata of society (Clark *et al.* 2014; Hellemans *et al.* 2014; Morrison 2006; WHO 2014; Women's Aid 2015). However, men and women, collectively and separately, have more access to resources and power in our society than infants and children. Some men and some women can and do abuse the power they have over their infants and children. The brilliance of feminist theory is how it challenges the status quo. This was originally in relation to the inequities between women and men, but more recently it has also been between women and women. Women of colour, of different sexual orientation and with disabilities have all expressed their experiences of being forgotten within a social movement intended to represent all women (Arnold & Ake 2013; Lehrner & Allen 2009).

Feminism today has changed. As a social worker, family therapist, infant mental health practitioner and feminist therapist, I identify with 'the values associated with the third wave, which embraces differences in others and advocates for respect and opportunity no matter an individual's gender, ethnicity, value sets, sexual orientation, and/or gender identity' (Blumer *et al.* 2010, p.70). This applies to my work with infants and children who experience oppression through being subjected to family violence, and who are not supported to have a voice in an area of practice which impacts them so profoundly.

> Feminist standpoint theory proposes that any theoretical framework that emerges from a 'general' standpoint will inevitably reflect only the reality of the dominant group and, as a result, will lead to practices that do not serve oppressed groups. Consequently, those who are oppressed will be in the best position to understand their reality and will be the ones best positioned to mobilize for informed, progressive change. (Arnold & Ake 2013, p.573)

Infants and children are a group oppressed by family violence which is not best served by the general 'standpoint' that operates in how we work and think within the family violence sector. It is not anti-feminist to ask for infants and children to be included in the debate involving how best to respond to tackling family violence.

LET'S BEGIN AGAIN

Working with infants and children to address family violence is confronting work. The coupling of infant- and child-led work with family violence work is stressful, not the least because workers are terrified that they may somehow intensify or exacerbate the level of risk the infant or child is exposed to. They may also fear that they are misreading situations, are not skilled enough, or are fearful of being targeted themselves by a perpetrator. Infant- and child-led work within the context of family violence is different to other work, in so far as the fear factor which comes into play inhibits reflective thinking. Notwithstanding the very real threat that may be posed by a perpetrator of family violence, it is more likely than not that the perpetrator uses the threat of violence, over the use of violence, to keep outsiders at bay. If we busily scurry off and look the other way when family violence is disclosed or indicated, we leave vulnerable infants, children and the non-offending parent alone to manage what will more likely be the use of violence, rather than simply the threat.

As workers, carers and service systems it is time we reflected on how we might approach family violence work differently. I offered my favourite quote in Chapter One (attributed to Goethe) in explaining how I approach undertaking this work: 'Whatever you can do or dream you can, begin it. Boldness has genius, power and magic in it' (Goethe 1808). Staying stuck and doing nothing as adults in response to family violence leaves infants and children in an impossible and perilous situation. What needs to change in this current equation is not the family members caught in this cycle of violence, but us. This takes us recognising 'the baby as having a mind and an intentional self from birth, who very early recognises his or her own body and feelings as different from those of others and who has capacity for empathy' (Thomson-Salo 2007, p.183). Infants will often seek connection with us, and we can offer them something meaningful by genuinely reciprocating and giving them a voice.

Talking to, thinking about, and advocating for infants and young children will require courage and boldness. However, being bold is not the same as being reckless. The risks we take are based on fundamental theories, concepts and scientific evidence that support working within relationships and through relationships. If we simply mirror back fear, numbness and futility, we will change nothing. If we believe in the hope that infants and children bring to the lives of parents and understand the brittleness and anxiety surrounding relationships fostered in fear, we can take a step back and reflect on bringing something new to the relationship (Morgan 2007).

Our baseline for ensuring the safety of infants and children needs to be strong and clear. What we do over and above this takes imagination, empathy, hopefulness and insight. Just as the infants and children we work with are 'not objects we do things to', neither should our approach to this work be limited to simply ensuring policies and procedures are tight and adhered to.

Infant- and child-led work is organic and the infant or young child is our teacher. Yes, their safety is paramount. What is missed in our interpretations of what makes the infant or child safe is often a consideration of their emotional world. This is because this is the hardest to measure and seemingly the most obscure and hardest to see. Rayna and Laevers (2011), speaking about early childhood education practices, declared that:

> we are now confirming and developing the image of the very young child as a rich and competent citizen...we must realize the enormous relevance of the insights coming from research on the under-3s...how much potential there is for a bottom-up movement where early years takes the lead. (p.169)

This statement can be equally applied to family violence work. The enormous amount of research and theory now available regarding 'infant mental health' provides powerful scientific evidence and compelling theoretical perspectives on how an individual's beginning in life powerfully informs their subsequent development. Understanding how we come to be through an 'infant mental health' perspective does not preclude respecting or integrating other important theoretical ideas, for example 'strengths based', 'feminist', 'narrative' or 'trauma informed' approaches.

Infant- and child-led approaches simply enlarge our field of vision to include the subjective experience of those so profoundly impacted at their age and stage in life by family violence. This infant and child (bottom-up) thinking, and the capacity for innovative services responses has not been mined with the same energy and commitment as has been afforded work with adults impacted by family violence. What do we have to lose in moving the infant and child more firmly into view in the way we work in, engage with and respond to this field of practice? What we could gain is enormous. It may bring something new into our response that offers more movement, hope, creativity and even delight to an issue in society that currently holds a place which is grim, stuck and all too often tragic.

Tips for Working with Infants (Bunston 2011)

Invite infants into your mind, your space and your interactions with their parents

This is done by being curious about the infant, what they are doing developmentally, how they express themselves, how much energy they give and how much they take. It is sometimes useful to wonder aloud in the presence of their parents and siblings, not asking rhetorical questions, but genuinely being curious about what it is the infant might be trying to communicate about their world. Taking time to wait and see what happens first, rather than rushing in to fill the space, can allow everyone time to think.

Do not overwhelm, do not underwhelm, infants

Being overbearing in your interactions with an infant impinges on their personal space as well as their developing self-agency. Under-interacting deprives the infant of opportunities for healthy stimulation and interaction. Learning the balance involves listening to and learning from the infant. The depressed infant may need encouragement to become more lively, while the anxious infant may need help modulating (or managing) their emotional states. Take your lead from the infant through observing them, how they interact with their parent and how they interact with you. If you find engaging with them hard work, that's probably a clue to how hard they find it engaging with you. Next question: is that coming from them, from you or somewhere in between?

Challenge the impulse to see infants as pre-verbal and thus not communicative

Watch with your eyes, your mind and your body. We have this funny idea that the most powerful communication comes through speech. Our earliest grasp on the world occurs non-verbally and, while research may suggest that more is communicated non-verbally than verbally, few of us tend to really believe this. How well we can manage our anxiety about 'not knowing' can reassure terribly anxious parents who feel like failures if they don't get it right the first time. Getting it right with an infant the 'first time' is not very realistic as infants themselves are very much exploring this brave new world of self and other/s. Being 'too sure' may lead to the mother who (for example) breastfeeds the infant every time they open their mouth, and which over time may override any other response, for both infant and mother.

Your entry point for change may in fact be the infant or child

As an adult centric society we can, without thinking, automatically defer all things (including asking a parent how a child is when the child is sitting right there with you) to the adults in the room. These adults may well be so caught up in their own trauma history and experiences of damaging relationships that shifts in thinking are difficult to achieve. While not in every case, most parents hold a hope for their infant's or child's future that is far more enlivened than for their own. A desire to be a different kind of parent or to provide a different future for their offspring is a powerful motivator. In other instances our capacity to simply see, engage with and delight in their children can offer parents a new and intriguing insight into what just 'might be' in their infant and within their relationship.

Do not under-estimate the power of play

Many adults have had very poor opportunities to play, but play is one of the first tools with which we explore the world and understand ourselves. Getting down and playing with the infants and children we work with and including their parents can bring about surprising results. Having a chance to sing, to draw, roll a ball, make a joke, rattle a tambourine, imagine a story with plastic tigers and dinosaurs, or dance about can all bypass one's usual patterns in responding and reveal, as well as allow opportunities to revel in other sensory experiences and ways of expressing. And as with all the other suggestions don't give up too fast. Doing new things takes time and persistence.

Keep it simple

Use cushions to sit on the floor to allow the infant or small child the opportunity to explore the space while you remain at their level. A minimum of toys is needed as too much over-stimulates and provides too great a distraction from the main event: watching the relationships between the parent or caregiver and the child. Gently reflect on what you see and don't be afraid to give voice to what you experience as painful feelings expressed by the infant through their behaviour and play. Try to keep the space and the toys, cushions and activities you may use consistent if you are to see this child over more than one session.

Keep it safe

Think about what is in the room within which you work which may be hazardous for a crawling or mobile infant or small child, for example, sharp corners, small objects, power points, steps. You will be amazed at what the child will find in your room which will fascinate them. If there is no harm, then let them explore. Bins full of papers make great crackling noises, can be sucked on and ripped up. Together, with their caregiver, work out what makes your room safe for their child. Importantly, this also includes how, and what is needed, to keep them emotionally and relationally safe. Talk to the infant directly, take your cues from them and tell them what you are doing and why. Also, be sure to ask for their permission, as you would the parent or caregiver. For example, 'is it ok if I touch your hand?' or in explaining why you might be taking something from them, 'I am taking this pencil away as it is sharp and may hurt you'. 'Maybe we can find something else that is fun and safe to play with?'

Recommended (and Rated) Further Reading

Brain development

The Body Keeps the Score: Brain, Mind, and Body in the Healing of Trauma by Bessel van der Kolk (Easy read)

Brain-Based Parenting by Daniel Hughes and Jonathon Baylin (Easy read)

Born for Love: Why Empathy is Essential and Endangered by Maia Szalavitz and Bruce D. Perry (Easy read)

The Boy who was Raised by a Dog by Bruce D. Perry and Maia Szalavitz (Easy read)

The Neuroscience of Human Relationships by Louis Cozolino (Easy to medium read)

Developing Mind: How Relationships and the Brain Interact to Shape who We Are by Daniel J. Siegel (Medium read)

Affect Regulation and the Origin of the Self: The Neurobiology of Emotional Development by Allan N. Schore (Comprehensive but difficult to read)

Infant mental health

The Interpersonal World of the Infant by Daniel Stern (Medium read)

The Handbook of Infant Mental Health edited by Charles H. Zeanah, Jr (Medium to difficult)

Parenthood and Mental Health edited by Sam Tyano, Miri Keren, Helen Herrman and John Cox (Medium)

The Baby as Subject by Campbell Paul and Frances Thomson-Salo (Easy to medium)

Winnicott: Playing and Reality by D.W. Winnicott (Medium to difficult)

Infants, children and violence and trauma

Don't Hit My Mommy! by Alicia F. Lieberman and Patricia Van Horn (Easy to medium)

Young Children and Trauma by Joy Osofsky (Easy to medium)

Domestic Violence and Protecting Children by Nicky Stanley and Cathy Humphreys (Easy to medium)

Children Who See Too Much by Betsy McAlister Groves (Easy)

When Father Kills Mother by Jean Harris-Hendriks, Dora Black and Tony Kaplan (Easy to medium)

Some helpful websites

World Association of Infant Mental Health
   www.waimh.org/i4a/pages/index.cfm?pageid=1

Zero to Three
   www.zerotothree.org

Brainwave Trust
www.brainwave.org.nz

The National Child Tramuatic Stress Network
www.nctsn.org/content/children-and-domestic-violence

Child Witness to Violence Project
www.childwitnesstoviolence.org

Child and Women Abuse Studies Unit
www.londonmet.ac.uk/research/centres/child-and-woman-abuse-studies-unit/

Australian Childhood Foundation
www.childhood.org.au

London Family Court Clinic (Canada)
www.lfcc.on.ca/

Child Development Institute
www.childdevelop.ca/programs/family-violence-services

Australian Fatherhood Research Bulletin
www.newcastle.edu.au/research-and-innovation/centre/fac/research

Group Work Interventions for Families Impacted by Family Violence

Below is a list of interventions I have been involved in developing for infants, children, their mothers and fathers impacted by family violence. Information about these interventions is available online at www.researchgate.net/profile/Wendy_Bunston.

The Peek a Boo Club™, for infants, toddlers and mothers who have experienced violence.

parkas (parents accepting responsibility kids are safe), for children (aged 8–12 years) and their mother who have experienced family violence.

BuBs (Building up Bonds) on Board, an early intervention program for infants and their mothers accessing crisis/emergency accommodation to escape family violence.

Dads on Board, for fathers who had successfully participated in a men's behaviour change program and their infant/toddler (up to age 4).

Feeling is Thinking (FisT), a school-based program for children aged 8–12 years who experience problems in expressing their strong feelings and who have difficulties in their interpersonal relationships.

Therapeutic Newsletters

Weekly therapeutic newsletters can serve many purposes in infant/ parent group work. Writing the newsletter provides facilitators with a process for clearly distilling what were the most salient issues that arose each session. They provide a powerful as well as tangible reminder of what happened each week, and can be kept as a reminder of the group's complete journey over the course of the program. The newsletter keeps participants who may have been unable to attend one session abreast of what happened that week. Importantly, the newsletter lets the participants know that we are keeping them in mind, and helps to keep the group experience within their mind. The newsletter is typically posted to arrive one or two days before the next group. The presentation is usually colourful, includes pictures and written in a manner which is inviting, chatty and meaningful. The voices of the infants or toddlers are prominent, as are the complexity of issues as explored by each group.

EXAMPLE ONE

Excerpt (minus pictures) taken directly from a therapeutic newsletter sent out weekly to mothers attending the Peek a Boo Club program, to a safe address as specified by each mother.

Week 3

This was our first week back post Melbourne Cup with (shockingly) no winners reported amongst the group! We were aware that Cecily and Lucy, and Mary and Annabel were not able to attend. We know sometimes there are complex and difficult things that are happening in people's lives. We are hopeful that they can return next week.

We had three toddler/mother dyads present, David and Karen, Ruby and May, and Sofie and Kylie. In the first half of the group the adults set the pace, and the space in the room exploring the issue of how do we answer questions from the children about their father's behaviour? We identified a dilemma between saying too little and saying too much and recognised that the infants and older children can struggle to make sense of what's happening around them.

The facilitators suggested that the children may need help to make sense of what's happening, and perhaps the answer is found somewhere in the middle!

One mother in the group gave a lovely example of how, when she was a child herself, her mother gave her too much of her own feelings about her father, using her as someone to offload on rather than helping make sense of her father's behaviour.

This led another mother to reflect on times when she felt she said too much, risking giving the child a bad impression of their dad. This seemed a tricky question which required us, as a group, to stop and think about just what our children are really asking us?

How can we explore how we communicate with our children? Maybe these are not quick question/answer talks but beginnings of life-long conversations.

And maybe we cannot always rely on words. Without words Ruby was persistent in letting her mum know what she wanted... her!

It was around this time that we noticed the children stayed very close to their mothers and, whilst keenly watching one another, dared not venture into the play space.

Karen wondered aloud, 'I wonder what the children would do if we stopped talking?' This led to us to pause and think. We have heard from you that this group is important in helping you clear your thoughts and be reflective...and before long we witnessed a transformation in the room. As we made less space for talking and more for observing the infants, they became much more visible, and active.

Sofie led the charge...crossing the room and picking up Ruby's shoes and then offering them back to her. Then she discovered one of the facilitor's (Mandy's) shoes and seemed very keen to try them on, or to try and be a grown-up girl.

It seemed to us that she wordlessly worked out, that if she could get back to the safe base of her mum, she could achieve her wish. As we wrote up this newsletter it led us to wonder how much could we learn if we simply watched?

The observant mood in the room seemed to allow the infants to be 'free to be playful!' The adults then mustered up enough courage to sing 'Glumpf goes the little green frog' and 'Open shut them'.

We then explored what songs we sang to our babies. May offered a rhyme she says to Ruby as she tickles her feet (and we all joined in numerous times): This little piggy goes to market, This little piggy stays home, This little piggy ate roast beef (is this good for a pig?) This little piggy had none, And this little piggy went wee wee wee all the way home!

And on that note...the children seem to now know the ritual of our good bye and feel safer in lying down under the stars fabric and the adults gently lifted it up and down above them whilst singing twinkle twinkle little star.

We wonder what it means to them to know the ritual now? Maybe that their world is predictable and safe for them, because their time with us has its own rhythm and thus is less worrying.

We are looking forward to seeing you all next week! *Need to reach us: Wendy, Mandy and Asha (phone numbers).*

EXAMPLE TWO
Except taken from a different Peek a Boo Club.

Week 8
This was our last week and lot of things happened and lots of emotions were felt. Emotionally the group began with a feeling of sadness at ending our time together and a disbelief that the eight weeks could go so fast. We, the facilitators, felt cross with ourselves that we had got the date of our last week of group wrong and for one mum and infant we even got the starting date wrong!

We also felt concern, worried for Tessa and Ivy as we had missed their presence over the last two weeks of group and hoped that everything was ok for them both. Brooke and Ivy were also unable to make it to the group and as had happened throughout this Peek a Boo group each week, it was almost like a new group with the mix of people attending changing nearly every week.

And as the mix of those people attending changed, so too did the opportunities to get to know one another. For one week, Amity and Tilley, perhaps our two quietest toddlers, had the space to themselves.

Maybe in keeping with the rather quiet mood of the group they both stayed close to their mothers for the first part of the group, Amity firmly ensconced in her mother's lap and Tilley, remaining close to Ashley, playing but watchful of everything that was happening around her. Tilley often sought contact with her mother, touching her shoulder or leg and then moving away.

Discussion was had about the children's fathers and the struggle between the heart and the head in their feelings for these men; giving them only a certain number of chances to prove their worthiness as partners and as fathers.

It was acknowledged that it took much strength to put the head first, choosing the welfare and safety of their children above what the heart may be feeling.

Whilst both mothers had made this choice, strong in their commitment to their babies, it also seemed it was a choice that left a sense of loneliness and sadness at times.

We spent some time exploring what the mothers and the infants had gotten out of coming to the Peek a Boo Club. One of the down sides was having to get up so early to get to the group!

Otherwise, the mothers felt it was a space where their stories could be heard and respected and that their infants got a great deal from playing with each other as well with their mothers.

The infants love the connection they have with their mothers and showed us this in various ways, Tilley imitating her mother in trying to juggle balls like her mother had and picking up her mum's hand bag when it was time to leave.

Amity clearly let us know 'it's my mum' in response to one of the facilitators offering Renata comfort by rubbing her back, and then Amity inviting Mum down onto the cushions for twinkle twinkle under the big silk stars fabric.

This constant, 24/7, role of being a mother was highlighted by both mums with the need to available always for their children as they are only very young. Both parents also acknowledged the need for some time for themselves as the children were getting old enough to be able to cope with this, with one mother joining her local gym and another looking at a return to school.

Half way through the group the mood in the room started to change. Tilley delighted in a game with Mum, where she was lifted up and down into the air and sung to, and then Amity and Jackie both came out to play a game of chasey.

One of the facilitators was almost chased off her feet as Amity and Tilley took turns to use the toy snake as the motivation for chasing and being chased – holding it out ahead of them and having much glee at the power it gave them!

This shift in the infants brought about a shift in the whole room with the remainder of the session becoming more playful. The baby dolls were rocked and sung to, put to bed and their nappies changed as well as being dressed, very imaginatively, in the material that makes up the cloth puppets.

And both girls were much more vocal, although not always easy to understand, and were certainly trying to communicate verbally. Whilst both struggle with their language skills at this point, their facial expressions, movements and actions have told us volumes about their world and how sometimes they feel happy, curious, playful and adventurous as well at other times they feel sad, uncertain, scared and thoughtful.

One thing is very clear – we will all miss the group, and we will all miss each other!

We will be in touch soon to make a suitable time to hold a reunion in the next month and to check in on how everyone is going.

Need to reach us: Wendy, Gemma, Hillary: (phone numbers).

References

Adamo, S.M.G. (2008) 'Observing educational relations in their natural context.' *Infant Observation 11*, 2, 131–146.

AIFS (2014) *Child Deaths from Abuse and Neglect*. Australia: Australian Institute of Family Studies. Available at www.aifs.gov.au/cfca/publications/child-deaths-abuse-and-neglect, accessed on 12 January 2017.

AIHW (2012a) *A Picture of Australia's Children 2012* (1742493572). (Cat. no. PHE 167.) Canberra: AIHW.

AIHW (2012b) *Specialist Homelessness Services Collection: First results, September Quarter 2011* (Cat. no. HOU 262.) Canberra: AIHW.

Allen, J., Fonagy, P. & Bateman, A.W. (2008) *Mentalizing in Clinical Practice*. Arlington, VA: American Psychiatric Publishing Inc.

Als, H., Tronick, E., Lester, B.M. & Brazelton, T.B. (1977) 'The Brazelton Neonatal Behavioral Assessment Scale (BNBAS).' *Journal of Abnormal Child Psychology 5*, 3, 215–229.

Ammaniti, M. & Gallese, V. (2014) *The Birth of Intersubjectivity: Psychodynamics, Neurobiology, and the Self*. New York: W.W. Norton & Company.

Anderson, K.M., Renner, L.M. & Danis, F.S. (2012) 'Recovery: Resilience and growth in the aftermath of domestic violence.' *Violence Against Women 18*, 11, 1279–1299.

Arnold, G. & Ake, J. (2013) 'Reframing the narrative of the battered women's movement.' *Violence Against Women 19*, 5, 557–578.

Bailey, B. & Eisikovits, Z. (2014) 'Violently reactive women and their relationship with an abusive mother.' *Journal of Interpersonal Violence 30*, 1, 1–24.

Baker, H. (2005) 'Involving children and young people in research on domestic violence and housing.' *Journal of Social Welfare and Family Law 27*, 3–4, 281–297.

Beebe, B. & Lachmann, F.M. (1998) 'Co-constructing inner and relational processes: Self-and mutual regulation in infant research and adult treatment.' *Psychoanalytic Psychology 15*, 4, 480–516.

Bick, E. (1964) 'Notes on infant observation in psycho-analytic training.' *The International Journal of Psycho-Analysis 45*, 558–566.

Bick, E. (1986) 'Further considerations on the function of the skin in early object relations.' *British Journal of Psychotherapy 2*, 4, 292–299.

Blumer, M.L.C., Green, M.S., Compton, D. & Barrera, A.M. (2010) 'Reflections on becoming feminist therapists: Honoring our feminist mentors.' *Journal of Feminist Family Therapy 22*, 1, 57–87.

Box, S.J., Copley, B., Magagna, J. & Moustaki, E. (1981) *Psychotherapy with Families: An Analytic Approach*. New York: Routledge.

Brazelton, T.B. & Nugent, J.K. (1995) *Neonatal Behavioral Assessment Scale* (3rd edition). London: Cambridge University Press.

Bretherton, I. (1991) 'The Roots and Growing Points of Attachment Theory.' In C.M. Parkes, J. Stevenson-Hinde & P. Marris (eds) *Attachment Across the Life Cycle*. London: Routledge.

Bunston, W. (2001) *Parkas: Parents Accepting Responsibility Kids are Safe*. Victoria, Australia: MHSKY.

Bunston, W. (2002) 'One way of responding to family violence – "putting on a PARKAS".' *Children Australia 27*, 4, 24–27.

Bunston, W. (2006) 'The Peek a Boo Club: Group work for infants and mothers affected by family violence.' *The Signal 14*, 1, 1–7.

Bunston, W. (2008a) 'Baby lead the way: Mental health groupwork for infants, children and mothers affected by family violence.' *Journal of Family Studies 14*, 2–1, 334–341.

Bunston, W. (2008b) 'Who's Left Holding the Baby: Infant-Led Systems Work in IPV.' In J. Hamel (ed.) *Intimate Partner Violence and Family Abuse.* New York: Springer Publishing Company.

Bunston, W. (2011) 'Let's start at the very beginning: The sound of infants, mental health, homelessness and you.' *Parity 24*, 2, 37–39. Available at http://search.informit.com.au/documentSummary;dn=908022936502962;res=IELFSC, accessed on 12 January 2017.

Bunston, W. (2013a) 'The Group who Holds the Group: Supervision as a Critical Component in a Group with Infants Affected by Family Violence.' In L.M. Grobman & J. Clements (eds) *Riding the Mutual Aid Bus and other Adventures in Group Work.* Harrisburg, PA: White Hat Communications.

Bunston, W. (2013b) '"What about the fathers?" bringing "Dads on Board™" with their infants and toddlers following violence.' *Journal of Family Studies 19*, 1, 70–79.

Bunston, W. (2015) 'Infant-Led Practice: Responding to Infants and their Mothers (and Fathers) in the Aftermath of Domestic Violence.' In N. Stanley & C. Humphreys (eds) *Domestic Violence and Protecting Children: New Thinking and Approaches.* London: Jessica Kingsley Publishers.

Bunston, W. (2016) *'How Refuge provides "refuge" to Infants: Exploring how "refuge" is provided to infants entering crisis accommodation with their mothers after fleeing family violence.'* PhD Thesis, La Trobe University. Melbourne. Available at http://hdl.handle.net/1959.9/559171, accessed on 12 January 2017.

Bunston, W. (2017) 'Children Exposed to Family Violence.' In C. Haen & S. Aronson (eds) *Handbook of Child and Adolescent Therapy.* New York: Routledge.

Bunston, W., Crean, H. & Thomson-Salo, F. (1999) *PARKAS (Parents Accepting Responsibility Kids are Safe).* VicGovernment–PADV. Melbourne, Victoria: P.G.P. Guides.

Bunston, W., Eyre, K., Carlsson, A. & Pringle, K. (2016) 'Evaluating relational repair work with infants and mothers impacted by family violence.' *Australian & New Zealand Journal of Criminology 49*, 1, 113–133.

Bunston, W. & Glennen, K. (2015) 'Holding the baby costs nothing.' *DVRCV Advocate, Spring/Summer,* 46–49.

Bunston, W. & Heynatz, A. (eds) (2006) *Addressing Family Violence Programs: Groupwork Interventions for Infants, Children and their Parents.* Victoria, Australia: Royal Children's Hospital Mental Health Service.

Bunston, W., Pavlidis, T. & Cartwright, P. (2016) 'Children, family violence and group work: Some do's and don'ts in running therapeutic groups with children affected by family violence.' *Journal of Family Violence 31*, 1, 85–94.

Bunston, W., Pavlidis, T. & Leyden, P. (2003) 'Putting the GRO into groupwork.' *Australian Social Work 56*, 1, 40–49.

Bunston, W. & Sketchley, R. (2012) *Refuge for Babies in Crisis.* Melbourne, Australia: RCH-IMHP. Available at www.salvationarmy.org.au/Global/State%20pages/Tasmania/Safe%20from%20the%20start/Refuge_for_Babies_Manual%20small.pdf, accessed on 12 January 2017.

Bürgin, D. (2011) 'From outside to inside to outside: Comments on intrapsychic representations and interpersonal interactions.' *Infant Mental Health Journal 32*, 1, 95–114.

Cacioppo, J.T. & Berntson, G.G. (1992) 'Social psychological contributions to the decade of the brain: Doctrine of multilevel analysis.' *American Psychologist 47*, 8, 1019–1028.

Calhoun, L.G. & Tedeschi, R.G. (2014) *Handbook of Posttraumatic Growth: Research and Practice.* New York: Psychology Press, Taylor & Francis Group.

Caron, N., Sobreira Lopes, R., Steibel, D. & Schneider Donelli, T. (2012) 'Writing as a challenge in the observer's journey through the Bick method of infant observation.' *Infant Observation 15*, 3, 221–230.

Chhabra, S. (2007) 'Physical violence during pregnancy.' *Journal of Obstetrics and Gynaecology 27*, 5, 460–463.

Chu, J. A. (1991) 'The repetition compulsion revisited: Reliving dissociated trauma.' *Psychotherapy: Theory, Research, Practice, Training 28*, 2, 327.

Clark, H.M., Galano, M.M., Grogan-Kaylor, A.C., Montalvo-Liendo, N. & Graham-Bermann, S.A. (2014) 'Ethnoracial variation in women's exposure to intimate partner violence.' *Journal of Interpersonal Violence 31*, 3, 1–22.

Cohen, N.J. (2006) 'Watch, wait, and wonder: An infant-led approach to infant-parent psychotherapy.' *The Signal 14*, 2, 1–4.

Cohen, N.J., Lojkasek, M., Muir, E., Muir, R. & Parker, C.J. (2002) 'Six-month follow-up of two mother–infant psychotherapies: Convergence of therapeutic outcomes.' *Infant Mental Health Journal 23*, 4, 361–380.

Cohen, N.J., Muir, E., Lojkasek, M., Muir, R., Parker, C.J., Barwick, M. & Brown, M. (1999) 'Watch, wait, and wonder: Testing the effectiveness of a new approach to mother-infant psychotherapy.' *Infant Mental Health Journal 20*, 4, 429–451.

Coll, C.G., Buckner, J.C., Brooks, M.G., Weinreb, L.F. & Bassuk, E.L. (1998) 'The developmental status and adaptive behavior of homeless and low-income housed infants and toddlers.' *American Journal of Public Health 88*, 9, 1371–1374.

Cory, G.A. (2002) 'Reappraising Macleans Triune Brain Concept.' In G.A. Cory & R. Gardner (eds) *The Evolutionary Neuroethology of Paul MacLean: Convergences and Frontiers*. Santa Barbara, CA: Praeger Publishers.

Cozolino, L. (2006) 'The social brain.' *Psychotherapy in Australia 12*, 2, 12–16.

Cozolino, L. (2008) 'It's a jungle in there.' *Psychotherapy Networker* (September/October).

Cozolino, L. (2014) *The Neuroscience of Human Relationships: Attachment and the Developing Social Brain.* New York: W.W. Norton & Company.

Crowell, J.A. & Treboux, D. (2006) 'A review of adult attachment measures: Implications for theory and research.' *Social Development 4*, 3, 294–327.

Dozier, M., Higley, E., Albus, K.E. & Nutter, A. (2002) 'Intervening with foster infants' caregivers: Targeting three critical needs.' *Infant Mental Health Journal 23*, 5, 541–554.

Emanuel, L. (2011) 'Brief interventions with parents, infants, and young children: A framework for thinking.' *Infant Mental Health Journal 32*, 6, 673–686.

Emery, R.E., Holtzworth-Munroe, A., Johnston, J.R., Pedro-Carroll, J.L. *et al.* (2016) '"Bending" Evidence for a Cause: Scholar-Advocacy Bias in Family Law.' *Family Court Review 54*, 2, 134–149.

FCA (2013) *Family Violence Best Practice Principles*. Canberra, ACT: Family Court of Australia.

Fleming, S. (2004) 'The contribution of psychoanalytical observation in child protection assessments.' *Journal of Social Work Practice 18*, 2, 223–238.

Fletcher, R.J. & StGeorge, J.M. (2010) 'Practitioners' understanding of father engagement in the context of family dispute resolution.' *Journal of Family Studies 16*, 2, 101–115.

Fonagy, P., Steele, M., Steele, H., Moran, G.S. & Higgitt, A.C. (1991) 'The capacity for understanding mental states: The reflective self in parent and child and its significance for security of attachment.' *Infant Mental Health Journal 12*, 3, 201–218.

Fortune, C.-A., Ward, T. & Polaschek, D. (2014) 'The Good Lives Model and therapeutic environments in forensic settings.' *Therapeutic Communities: The International Journal of Therapeutic Communities 35*, 3, 95–104.

Fraiberg, S., Adelson, E. & Shapiro, V. (1975) 'Ghosts in the nursery.' *Journal of the American Academy of Child Psychiatry 14*, 3, 387–421.

Friedman, S.H., Hrouda, D.R., Holden, C.E., Noffsinger, S.G. & Resnick, P.J. (2005) 'Filicide-suicide: Common factors in parents who kill their children and themselves.' *Journal of the American Academy of Psychiatry and the Law Online 33*, 4, 496–504.

Fromm, E. (1968/2010) *The Revolution of Hope: Toward a Humanized Technology.* New York: American Mental Health Foundation Books.

Garcia-Moreno, C., Jansen, H.A., Ellsberg, M., Heise, L. & Watts, C.H. (2006) 'Prevalence of intimate partner violence: Findings from the WHO multi-country study on women's health and domestic violence.' *The Lancet 368*, 9543, 1260–1269.

Gazmararian, J.A., Petersen, R., Spitz, A.M., Goodwin, M.M., Saltzman, L.E. & Marks, J.S. (2000) 'Violence and reproductive health: Current knowledge and future research directions.' *Maternal and Child Health Journal 4*, 2, 79–84.

Glennen, K. (2011) 'The homeless infant.' *Parity 24*, 2, 35–36.

Goethe, J.W. v. (1808) *Faust – Part One* (trans. George Madison Priest). Cambridge: University Press: Welch, Bigelow, and Company. Available at https://web.archive.org/web/20130331154558/http://www.einam.com/faust/index.html, accessed on 31 January 2017.

Golding, P. & Fitzgerald, H.E. (2016) 'Trauma and boys: What's different?' *ZERO TO THREE 36*, 5, 12–21.

Goldner, V., Penn, P., Sheinberg, M. & Walker, G. (1990) 'Love and violence: Gender paradoxes in volatile attachments.' *Family Process 29*, 4, 343–364.

Gondolf, E.W. (1988) 'The effect of batterer counseling on shelter outcome.' *Journal of Interpersonal Violence 3*, 3, 275–289.

Goodmark, L. (1999) 'From property to personhood: What the legal system should do for children in family violence cases.' *West Virginia Law Review 102*, 237–338.

Graham, A.M., Fisher, P.A. & Pfeifer, J.H. (2013) 'What sleeping babies hear: A functional MRI study of interparental conflict and infants' emotion processing.' *Psychological Science 24*, 5, 782–789.

Harcourt, D. & Einarsdottir, J. (2011) 'Introducing children's perspectives and participation in research.' *European Early Childhood Education Research Journal 19*, 3, 301–307.

Hellemans, S., Loeys, T., Buysse, A. & De Smet, O. (2014) 'Prevalence and impact of intimate partner violence (IPV) among an ethnic minority population.' *Journal of Interpersonal Violence 30*, 19, 3389–3418.

Hesse, E. & Main, M. (2006) 'Frightened, threatening, and dissociative parental behavior in low-risk samples: Description, discussion, and interpretations.' *Development and Psychopathology 18*, 2, 309–343.

Hoffman, K.T., Marvin, R.S., Cooper, G. & Powell, B. (2006) 'Changing toddlers' and preschoolers' attachment classifications: The circle of security intervention.' *Journal of Consulting and Clinical Psychology 74*, 6, 1017–1026.

Holmes, J. (1993) *John Bowlby and Attachment Theory*. London: Routledge.

Hughes, J., Corbally, M. & Kelowna, B. (2014) 'Over-Researched and Under-Theorized: Re-imagining the Concept of Gender for Intimate Partner Violence Theory and Research.' In A.M. Columbus (ed.) *Advances In Psychology Research* (Vol. 100). New York: Nova Science Publishers.

Hughes, M. & Heycox, K. (2005) 'Promoting reflective practice with older people: Learning and teaching strategies.' *Australian Social Work 58*, 4, 344–356.

Humphreys, C., Thiara, R.K. & Skamballis, A. (2011) 'Readiness to change: Mother–child relationship and domestic violence intervention.' *British Journal of Social Work 41*, 1, 166–184.

IFVPF (2008) *Strong Culture, Strong Peoples, Strong Families Towards a safer future for Indigenous families and communities*. Melbourne, Victoria: Aboriginal Affairs Victoria. Available at www.dhs.vic.gov.au/__data/assets/pdf_file/0012/620202/Final_10_Year_Plan_Oct08_2nd_Edition.pdf, accessed on 13 January 2017.

Jaremka, L.M., Glaser, R., Loving, T.J., Malarkey, W.B., Stowell, J.R. & Kiecolt-Glaser, J.K. (2013) 'Attachment anxiety is linked to alterations in cortisol production and cellular immunity.' *Psychological Science 24*, 3, 272–279.

Jones, S. & Bunston, W. (2012) 'The" original couple": Enabling mothers and infants to think about what destroys as well as engenders love, when there has been intimate partner violence.' *Couple and Family Psychoanalysis 2*, 2, 215–232.

Jordan, B. (2011) 'Focusing the lens: The infant's point of view. Discussion of "Brief interventions with parents, infants, and young children: A framework for thinking".' *Infant Mental Health Journal 32*, 6, 687–693.

Jordan, B. (2012) 'Therapeutic play within infant–parent psychotherapy and the treatment of infant feeding disorders.' *Infant Mental Health Journal 33*, 3, 307–313.

Jordan, B. & Sketchley, R. (2009) 'A stich in time saves nine.' Melbourne, Australia: V. Press. (30). Available at www.aifs.gov.au/nch/pubs/issues/issues30/issues30.html, accessed on 17 January 2017.

Labarre, M., Bourassa, C., Holden, G.W., Turcotte, P. & Letourneau, N. (2016) 'Intervening with fathers in the context of intimate partner violence: An analysis of ten programs and suggestions for a research agenda.' *Journal of Child Custody 13*, 1, 1–29.

Lambert, K.G. (2003) 'The life and career of Paul MacLean: A journey toward neurobiological and social harmony.' *Physiology & Behavior 79*, 3, 343–349.

Lehrner, A. & Allen, N.E. (2009) 'Still a movement after all these years?: Current tensions in the domestic violence movement.' *Violence Against Women 15*, 6, 656–677.

Letourneau, N., Young Morris, C., Secco, L., Stewart, M., Hughes, J. & Critchley, K. (2013) 'Mothers and infants exposed to intimate partner violence compensate.' *Violence and Victims 28*, 4, 571–586.

Levendosky, A.A., Bogat, G.A., Huth-Bocks, A.C., Rosenblum, K. & Von Eye, A. (2011) 'The effects of domestic violence on the stability of attachment from infancy to preschool.' *Journal of Clinical Child & Adolescent Psychology 40*, 3, 398–410.

Lieberman, A.F., Padrón, E., Van Horn, P. & Harris, W.W. (2005) 'Angels in the nursery: The intergenerational transmission of benevolent parental influences.' *Infant Mental Health Journal 26*, 6, 504–520.

Luijk, M.P.C.M., Roisman, G.I., Haltigan, J.D., Tiemeier, H. *et al.* (2011) 'Dopaminergic, serotonergic, and oxytonergic candidate genes associated with infant attachment security and disorganization? In search of main and interaction effects.' *Journal of Child Psychology and Psychiatry 52*, 12, 1295–1307.

MacLean, P.D. (1982) 'On the Origin and Progressive Evolution of the Triune Brain.' In E. Armstrong & D. Falk (eds) *Primate Brain Evolution: Methods and Concepts*. New York: Plenum Press.

MacLean, P.D. (1990) *The Truine Brain in Evolution*. New York: Plenum Press.

Maillard, K.N. (2010) 'Rethinking children as property: The transitive family.' *Cardozo Law Review 32*, 1, 101–141.

Maillard, K.N. (2012) *Rethinking Children as Property*. College of Law Faculty Scholarship, Paper 75. Available at http://surface.syr.edu/lawpub/75, accessed on 13 January 2017.

Main, M. (1991) 'Metacognitive Knowledge, Metacognitive Monitoring, and Singular (Coherent) vs. Multiple (Incoherent) Model of Attachment.' In C.M. Parkes, J. Stevenson-Hinde & P. Marris (eds) *Attachment Across the Life Cycle*. London: Routledge

Main, M. (1999) 'Attachment Theory: Eighteen Points with Suggestions for Future Studies.' In J. Cassidy & P.R. Shaver (eds) *Handbook of Attachment: Theory, Research, and Clinical Implications*. New York: Guildford Press.

Main, M. & Hesse, E. (1990) 'Parents' Unresolved Traumatic Experiences are Related to Infant Disorganized Attachment Status: Is Frightened and/or Frightening Parental Behavior the Linking Mechanism?' In M.T. Greenberg, D. Cicchetti & E.M. Cummings (eds) *Attachment in the Preschool Years: Theory, Research, and Intervention*. Chicago, IL: The University of Chicago Press.

Main, M., Kaplan, N. & Cassidy, J. (1985) 'Security in infancy, childhood, and adulthood: A move to the level of representation.' *Monographs of the Society for Research in Child Development 50*, 1/2, 66–104.

Main, M. & Solomon, J. (1990) 'Procedures for Identifying Infants as Disorganized/Disoriented during the Ainsworth Strange Situation.' In M.T. Greenberg, D. Cicchetti & E.M. Cummings (eds) *Attachment in the Preschool Years: Theory, Research, and Intervention*. Chicago, IL: The University of Chicago Press.

Martinez-Torteya, C., Bogat, G.A., Von Eye, A. & Levendosky, A.A. (2009) 'Resilience among children exposed to domestic violence: The role of risk and protective factors.' *Child Development 80*, 2, 562–577.

Marvin, R., Cooper, G., Hoffman, K. & Powell, B. (2002) 'The circle of security project: Attachment-based intervention with caregiver-pre-school child dyads.' *Attachment & Human Development 4*, 1, 107–124.

Masten, A.S. (2011) 'Resilience in children threatened by extreme adversity: Frameworks for research, practice, and translational synergy.' *Development and Psychopathology 23*, 2, 493–506.

McFarlane, J., Malecha, A., Gist, J., Watson, K. *et al.* (2005) 'Intimate partner sexual assault against women and associated victim substance use, suicidality, and risk factors for femicide.' *Issues in Mental Health Nursing 26*, 9, 953–967.

McGilchrist, I. (2011) 'Paying attention to the bipartite brain.' *The Lancet 377*, 9771, 1068–1069.

McKenzie-Smith, S. (2009) 'Observational study of the elderly: An applied study utilizing Esther Bick's infant observation technique.' *Infant Observation 12*, 1, 107–115.

McMillan, R., Kaufman, S.B. & Singer, J.L. (2013) 'Ode to positive constructive daydreaming.' *Frontiers in Psychology 4*, 626, 1–9.

Meares, R. (1993) *The Metaphor of Play: Disruption and Restoration in the Borderline Experience.* New York: Jason Aronson Inc.

Meltzoff, A.N. & Moore, M.K. (1983) 'Newborn infants imitate adult facial gestures.' *Child Development 54*, 3, 702–709.

Menezes-Cooper, T. (2013) 'Domestic violence and pregnancy: A literature review.' *International Journal of Childbirth Education 28*, 3, 30–33.

Moore, T., McArthur, M., Noble-Carr, D. & Harcourt, D. (2015) *Taking Us Seriously: Children and Young People Talk about Safety and Institutional Responses to their Safety Concerns.* Canberra: A. C. University.

Morgan, A. (2007) 'What Am I Trying to Do When I See the Infant with his or her Parents.' In F.T. Salo & C. Paul (eds) *The Baby as Subject* (2nd edition). Melbourne: Stonnington Press.

Morrison, Z. (2006) *Results of the Personal Safety Survey 2005.* Australia: AIFS.

Muir, E., Lojkasek, M. & Cohen, N.J. (1999) 'Watch, wait, & wonder: A manual describing a dyadic infant-led approach to problems in infancy and early-childhood.' *Infant Mental Health Journal 20*, 4, 429–451.

Neave, M., Faulkner, P. & Nicholson, T. (2016) *Royal Commission into Family Violence: Report and Recommendations.* Victoria: Australia Victorian Government Printer.

Newman, J. & Harris, J. (2009) 'The scientific contributions of Paul D. MacLean (1913–2007).' *Journal of Nervous & Mental Disease 197*, 1, 3–5.

Nicolson, S. (2015) 'Let's meet your baby as a person: From research to preventative perinatal practice and back again, with the newborn behavioral observations.' *ZERO TO THREE*, September, 28–39.

Nugent, J.K., Keefer, C.H., Minear, S., Johnson, L.C. & Blanchard, Y. (2007) *Understanding Newborn Behaviour and Early Relationships.* Baltimore, MD: Paul H Brookes Publishing Company.

Ombudsman (2015) *Investigation into issues associated with violence restraining orders and their relationship with family and domestic violence fatalities.* Western Australia Ombudsman Office. Available at www.ombudsman.wa.gov.au/Publications/Documents/reports/FDVROs/FDVRO-Investigation-Report-191115.pdf, accessed on 31 January 2017.

Osofsky, J.D. (2003) 'Prevalence of children's exposure to domestic violence and child maltreatment: Implications for prevention and intervention.' *Clinical Child and Family Psychology Review 6*, 3, 161–170.

Paul, C. (2007) 'Infants Born of a Rape.' In F.T. Salo & C. Paul (eds) *The Baby as Subject* (2nd edition). Melbourne: Stonnington Press.

Paul, C. & Thomson-Salo, F. (2014) *The Baby as Subject: Clinical Studies in Infant–Parent Therapy.* London: Karnac Books.

Perry, B., Pollard, R., Blakley, T., Baker, W. & Vigilante, D. (1995) 'Childhood trauma, the neurobiology of adaptation, and "use-dependent" development of the brain: How "states" become "traits".' *Infant Mental Health Journal 16*, 4, 271–291.

Perry, B. & Szalavitz, M. (2006) *The Boy Who Was Raised as a Dog.* New York: Basic Books.

Perry, B.D. (1997) 'Incubated in Terror: Neurodevelopmental Factors in the "Cycle of violence".' In J. Osofsky (ed.) *Children in a Violent Society.* New York: The Guilford Press.

Perry, B.D. (2005) *Maltreatment and the Developing Child.* Ontario, Canada. Available at www.childtrauma.org/wp-content/uploads/2013/11/McCainLecture_Perry.pdf, accessed on 13 January 2017.

Pinheiro, P.S. (2006) *World Report on Violence Against Children.* Switzerland: UN.

Porges, S.W. (2015) 'Making the world safe for our children: Down-regulating defence and up-regulating social engagement to "optimise" the human experience.' *Children Australia 40*, Special Issue 02, 114–123.

Powell, B., Cooper, G., Hoffman, K. & Marvin, B. (2013) *The Circle of Security Intervention: Enhancing Attachment in Early Parent–Child Relationships.* New York: The Guilford Press.

Quinlivan, J.A. & Evans, S. (2005) 'Impact of domestic violence and drug abuse in pregnancy on maternal attachment and infant temperament in teenage mothers in the setting of best clinical practice.' *Archives of Women's Mental Health 8*, 3, 191–199.

Rasool, S. (2015) 'Help-seeking after domestic violence: The critical role of children.' *Journal of Interpersonal Violence 31*, 9, 1661–1686.

Rayna, S. & Laevers, F. (2011) 'Understanding children from 0 to 3 years of age and its implications for education. What's new on the babies' side? Origins and evolutions.' *European Early Childhood Education Research Journal 19*, 2, 161–172.

Rechner, A. (2016) [Translation.] Personal Correspondence. Melbourne.

Reddy, V. & Trevarthen, C. (2004) 'What we learn about babies from engaging their emotions.' *ZERO TO THREE 24*, 3, 9–15.

Rifkin-Graboi, A., Borelli, J.L. & Enlow, M.B. (2009) 'Neurobiology of Stress in Infancy.' In C.H. Zeanah Jr (ed.) *Handbook of Infant Mental Health* (3rd edition). New York: The Guilford Press.

Rothschild, B. (2000) *The Body Remembers: The Psychophysiology of Trauma and Trauma Treatment.* New York: W.W. Norton & Company.

Rustin, M. (2006) 'Infant observation research: What have we learned so far?' *Infant Observation 9*, 1, 35–52.

Rustin, M. (2009) 'Esther Bick's legacy of infant observation at the Tavistock – some reflections 60 years on.' *Infant Observation 12*, 1, 29–41.

Ryan, G. (1989) 'Victim to victimizer: Rethinking victim treatment.' *Journal of Interpersonal Violence 4*, 3, 325–341.

Ryan, G.D. & Lane, S.L. (1997) 'Integrating Theory and Method.' In G.D. Ryan & S.L. Lane (eds) *Juvenile Sexual Offending: Causes, Consequences, and Correction.* San Francisco, CA: Jossey-Bass.

Salter-Ainsworth, M.D. & Bowlby, J. (1991) 'An ethological approach to personality development.' *American Psychologist 46*, 4, 333–341.

Salter-Ainsworth, M.D. & Eichberg, C. (1991) 'Effects on Infant–Mother Attachment of Mother's Unresolved Loss of an Attachment Figure, or Other Traumatic Experience.' In C.M. Parkes, J. Stevenson-Hinde & P. Marris (eds) *Attachment Across The Life Cycle* (Vol. 3). London: Routledge.

Schechter, D.S. & Willheim, E. (2009) 'The Effects of Violent Experiences on Infants and Young Children.' In C.H. Zeanah Jr (ed.) *Handbook of Infant Mental Health.* New York: The Guilford Press.

Schore, A.N. (2001a) 'Contributions from the decade of the brain to infant mental health: An overview.' *Infant Mental Health Journal 22*, 1–2, 1–6.

Schore, A.N. (2001b) 'The effects of early relational trauma on right brain development, affect regulation, and infant mental health.' *Infant Mental Health Journal 22*, 1–2, 201–269.

Schore, A.N. (2003a) *Affect Dysregulation and Disorders of the Self.* New York: W.W. Norton & Company.

Schore, A.N. (2003b) *Affect Regulation and the Repair of the Self* (Vol. 2). New York: W.W. Norton & Company.

Schore, A.N. (2005) 'Back to basics attachment, affect regulation, and the developing right brain: Linking developmental neuroscience to pediatrics.' *Pediatrics in Review 26*, 6, 204–217.

Schore, A.N. (2016) *Affect Regulation and the Origin of the Self: The Neurobiology of Emotional Development.* New York: Routledge.

Schore, J.R. & Schore, A.N. (2008) 'Modern attachment theory: The central role of affect regulation in development and treatment.' *Clinical Social Work Journal 36*, 1, 9–20.

Shatz, C. (1992) 'The developing brain.' *Scientific American 267*, 3, 35–41.

Shinn, M. (2010) 'Homelessness, poverty, and social exclusion in the U.S. and Europe.' *European Journal on Homelessness 4*, 21–44.

Siegel, D.J. (2001) 'Toward an interpersonal neurobiology of the developing mind: Attachment relationships, "mindsight," and neural integration.' *Infant Mental Health Journal 22*, 1–2, 67–94.

Siegel, D.J. (2012) *Developing Mind: How Relationships and the Brain Interact to Shape Who We Are* (2nd edition). New York: Guilford Press.

Singer, J. (2002) 'Cognitive and Affective Implications of Imaginative Play in Childhood.' In M. Lewis (ed.) *Child and Adolescent Psychiatry: A Comprehensive Textbook* (3rd edition). Philadelphia, PA: Lippincott Williams & Wilkins.

Slade, A. (1994) 'Making Meaning and Making Believe: Their Role in the Clinical Process.' In A. Slade & D. Wolf (eds) *Children at Play: Clinical and Developmental Approaches to Meaning and Representation.* New York: Oxford University Press.

Stafford, A. (2016) 'Into darkness.' *The Age,* March 12. Available at www.smh.com.au/national/my-friend-who-killed-her-daughter-20160224-gn2j5v.html, accessed on 31 January 2017.

Stern, D.N. (2003) *The Interpersonal World of the Infant: A View from Psychoanalysis and Developmental Psychology.* London: Karnac Books.

Stolorow, R. (1994) 'The intersubjective context of intrapsychic experience.' In R. Stolorow, G. Atwood & B. Brandchaft (eds) *The Intersubjective Perspective.* New York: Aronson.

Stone, J. (2016) 'The Necessary Loom: Finding our way as an infant mental health practioner.' Paper presented at the AAIMHI-WA, Western Australia.

Talge, N.M., Neal, C. & Glover, V. (2007) 'Antenatal maternal stress and long-term effects on child neurodevelopment: How and why?' *Journal of Child Psychology and Psychiatry 48*, 3–4, 245–261.

Teicher, M.H. (2002) 'Scars that won't heal.' *Scientific American 286*, 3, 68–75.

Teicher, M.H., Andersen, S.L., Polcari, A., Anderson, C.M., Navalta, C.P. & Kim, D.M. (2003) 'The neurobiological consequences of early stress and childhood maltreatment.' *Neuroscience & Biobehavioral Reviews 27*, 1–2, 33–44.

Teicher, M.H., Dumont, N.L., Ito, Y., Vaituzis, C., Giedd, J.N. & Andersen, S.L. (2004) 'Childhood neglect is associated with reduced corpus callosum area.' *Biological Psychiatry 56*, 2, 80–85.

Thiel de Bocanegra, H., Rostovtseva, D.P., Khera, S. & Godhwani, N. (2010) 'Birth control sabotage and forced sex: Experiences reported by women in domestic violence shelters.' *Violence Against Women 16*, 5, 601–612.

Thomson-Salo, F. (2007) 'Relating to the Infant as Subject in the Context of Family Violence.' In F. Thomson-Salo & C. Paul (eds) *The Baby as Subject* (2nd edition). Victoria, Australia: Stonnington Press.

Thomson-Salo, F. (2010) 'Parenting an Infant Born of Rape.' In S. Tyano, M. Keren, H. Herrman & J. Cox (eds) *Parenthood and Mental Health: A Bridge between Infant and Adult Psychiatry.* Oxford: Wiley-Blackwell.

Thomson-Salo, F. (2014) 'A Preventive Attachment Intervention with Adolescent Mothers: Elaboration of the Intervention.' In R.N. Emde & M. Leuzinger-Bohleber (eds) *Early Parenting and Prevention of Disorder: Psychoanalytic Research at Interdisciplinary Frontiers.* London: Karnac Books.

Thomson-Salo, F., Paul, C., Morgan, A., Jones, S. *et al.* (1999) '"Free to be playful": Therapeutic work with infants.' *Infant Observation 3*, 1, 47–62.

Tolan, P., Gorman-Smith, D. & Henry, D. (2006) 'Family violence.' *Annual Review of Psychology 57*, January, 557–583.

Trevarthen, C. (2001) 'Intrinsic motives for companionship in understanding their origin, development, and significance for infant mental health.' *Infant Mental Health Journal 22*, 1–2, 95–131.

Tronick, E. & Beeghly, M. (2011) 'Infants' meaning-making and the development of mental health problems.' *American Psychologist 66*, 2, 107–119.

Tronick, E.Z. (2001) 'Emotional connections and dyadic consciousness in infant-mother and patient-therapist interactions: Commentary on paper by Frank M. Lachmann.' *Psychoanalytic Dialogues 11*, 2, 187–194.

Tronick, E.Z. (2007) The *Neurobehavioral and Social-Emotional Development of Infants and Children*. New York: W.W. Norton & Company.

Uddin, L.Q., Iacoboni, M., Lange, C. & Keenan, J.P. (2007) 'The self and social cognition: The role of cortical midline structures and mirror neurons.' *Trends in Cognitive Sciences 11*, 4, 153–157.

Van der Kolk, B. A. (1989) 'The compulsion to repeat the trauma.' *Psychiatric Clinics of North America 12*, 2, 389–411.

Van der Kolk, B. (2014) *The Body Keeps the Score: Brain, Mind, and Body in the Healing of Trauma*. London: Penguin.

Vázquez, C. (2013) 'A New Look at Trauma: From Vulnerability Models to Resilience and Positive Changes.' In K.A. Moore, K. Kaniasty, P. Buchwald & A. Sese (eds) *Stress and Anxiety: Applications to Health and Wellbeing, Work Stressors and Assessment*. Berlin: Logos Verlag.

Walker, L. (1979) *The Battered Woman*. New York: Harper & Row.

Waller, T. & Bitou, A. (2011) 'Research with children: Three challenges for participatory research in early childhood.' *European Early Childhood Education Research Journal 19*, 1, 5–20.

WHO (2009) *Violence Prevention: The Evidence*. Geneva: WHO. Available at http://apps.who.int/iris/bitstream/10665/77936/1/9789241500845_eng.pdf?ua=1, accessed on 31 January 2017.

WHO (2013) *Global and Regional Estimates of Violence Against Women*. Geneva: WHO.

WHO (2014) *Global Status Report on Violence Prevention 2014*. Luxembourg: WHO.

Winnicott, D. (1960) 'The theory of the parent–infant relationship.' *International Journal of Psychoanalysis 41*, 585–595.

Women's Aid (2015) *Women's Aid Annual Survey 2014*. Cardigan, UK: Women's Aid.

Yehuda, R. (2004) 'Risk and resilience in posttraumatic stress disorder.' *Journal of Clinical Psychiatry 65* (suppl. 1), 29–36.

Subject Index

Author Index

Dr Wendy Bunston has been working with children in recovery from family violence for over 25 years. She has worked as a senior social worker and as a manager and senior clinician at Melbourne's Royal Children's Hospital Mental Health Program. She is a qualified infant mental health worker and member of the Australian Association of Infant Mental Health. After receiving several awards for her work, including the 2006 and 2010 Australian Crime and Violence Prevention Awards, Wendy completed a PhD in Refuge for Infants and their Mothers After Leaving Family Violence at La Trobe University. Her thesis, entitled *How Refuge Provides 'refuge' for Infants*, received the 2016 Nancy Millis Award, and can be found at http://hdl.handle.net/1959.9/559171.